GCSE Edexcel
Additional Science
Higher Workbook

This book is for anyone doing **GCSE Edexcel Additional Science** at higher level.
It covers everything you'll need for your year 11 exams.

It's full of **tricky questions**... each one designed to make you **sweat**
— because that's the only way you'll get any **better**.

There are questions to see **what facts** you know. There are questions
to see how well you can **apply those facts**. And there are questions
to see what you know about **how science works**.

It's also got some daft bits in to try and make the whole
experience at least vaguely entertaining for you.

<u>What CGP is all about</u>

Our sole aim here at CGP is to produce the highest
quality books — carefully written, immaculately presented
and dangerously close to being funny.

Then we work our socks off to get them
out to you — at the cheapest possible prices.

Contents

Published by CGP

Editors:
Luke Antieul, Charlotte Burrows, Mary Falkner, Helena Hayes, Felicity Inkpen,
Rosie McCurrie, Jane Sawers, Karen Wells, Sarah Williams.

Contributors:
Steve Coggins, Jane Davies, Max Fishel, James Foster, Paddy Gannon, Dr Giles R Greenway,
Dr Iona M J Hamilton, Rebecca Harvey, Frederick Langridge, Sidney Stringer Community School,
Chris Workman.

ISBN: 978 1 84762 769 8

With thanks to Helen Brace, Barrie Crowther, Cathy Davis, Ben Fletcher, Edmund Robinson
and Karen Wells for the proofreading.

With thanks to Jan Greenway, Laura Jakubowski and Laura Stoney for the copyright research.

Every effort has been made to locate copyright holders and obtain permission to reproduce
sources. For those sources where it has been difficult to trace the originator of the work,
we would be grateful for information. If any copyright holder would like us to make an
amendment to the acknowledgements, please notify us and we will gladly update the book at
the next reprint. Thank you.

Groovy website: www.cgpbooks.co.uk

Printed by Elanders Ltd, Newcastle upon Tyne.
Jolly bits of clipart from CorelDRAW®
Based on the classic CGP style created by Richard Parsons.

Cells and Microscopy

Q1 Plant and animal cells have **similarities** and **differences**.
Complete each statement below by circling the correct words.

a) (Plant) / Animal cells, but not **plant** / (animal) cells, contain chloroplasts.

b) Plant cells have (vacuoles) / **cytoplasm** containing cell sap.

c) (Both plant and animal cells) / Only plant cells / Only animal cells have cell membranes.

d) The (cytoplasm) / **nucleus** is the gel-like part of the cell, where most of the chemical reactions happen.

Q2 Draw lines to match up each **part** of a bacterium to its correct **description**.

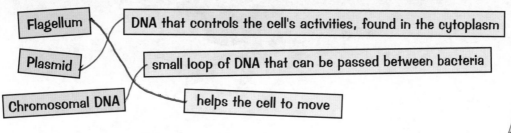

Flagellum

Plasmid

Chromosomal DNA

DNA that controls the cell's activities, found in the cytoplasm

small loop of DNA that can be passed between bacteria

helps the cell to move

Q3 This question is about the **parts** of a cell.

a) State what each of the following cell structures contains or is made of.

   i) The **nucleus** contains ..DNA..

   ii) **Chloroplasts** contain ...cytoplasm which is key in photosynthe..

   iii) The **cell wall** is made of ...celulose..

b) Describe the functions of these parts of the cell.

   i) The **nucleus** ..contains the DNA responsable for the func..

   ii) **Chloroplasts** ..sites of photosynthesis......................................

   iii) The **cell wall** ....

   iv) The **cell membrane** ....

   v) **Mitochondria** ....

Q4 The diagram shows a typical **bacterium**.

a) Name parts A and B on the diagram.

   A ..DNA..

   B ..Cell wall..

b) Name **one** feature of a typical plant cell that is not seen in bacterial cells.

   ....

Cells and Microscopy

Q5   **Microscopes** let us see things that we can't see with the naked eye.

a) A picture of a light microscope is shown below.

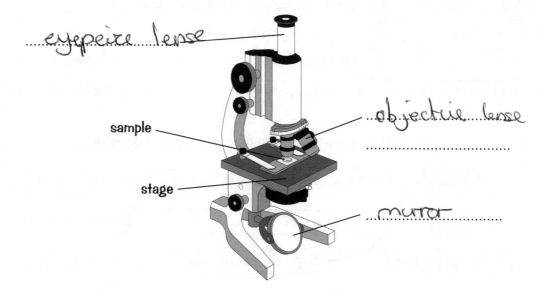

.....eyepeice.....lense

...objectiue.....lense

sample

stage

.....murror

i) Complete the missing labels on the picture of the microscope.

ii) Circle the parts of the microscope you would use to focus your image.

b) Name **two** plant cell structures that you'd be able to see using a light microscope.

1. ...Cell....wall...

2. .....Cell....membrane..

c) Name **one** type of microscope, other than a light microscope.

...electron......microscope..

Q6   Professor Smart has invented a shrinking ray. He tests it on his cat, Fluffy, by shrinking him down to **0.06 mm long**.

a) The Professor looks at Fluffy using a **light microscope**. The image that he sees is **9 mm long**. Calculate the magnification of Professor Smart's image.

....

....

b) Fluffy's tail is **0.02 mm** long. The Professor now looks at him using **× 300** magnification. Calculate how long Fluffy's tail will be on the magnified image.

....

....

DNA

Q1 The following questions are about **DNA**.

a) What name is given to the shape of a DNA molecule? ...Double helix...

b) How many different **bases** are there in DNA? ......8 4...

c) Which bases pair up together?

......A + T, T + A, G + C, C + G......

d) What type of bonds hold the base pairs together? ...weak hydrogen bonds...

Q2 You can extract **DNA** from **onion cells** in a simple experiment in the lab.

a) The steps of this experiment are shown below.
Put them in the correct order by numbering the boxes. The first one has been done for you.

5	Cool the mixture down again and filter it.
4	Put the beaker into a water bath at 60 °C for 15 minutes.
6	Add ice-cold alcohol to the filtered mixture. When the DNA has come out of solution, fish it out using a glass rod.
1	Chop the onion. Put it in a beaker with a solution of detergent and salt.
3	Once the mixture is ice-cold, put it into a blender for a few seconds.
2	Put the beaker in ice to cool the mixture down.

b) Explain why the mixture is heated to 60 °C for 15 minutes.

...To help it seperate out...

Q3 Complete the passage about the **discovery of DNA** using some of the words below.

| light   equal to   Rosalind Franklin   X-rays   Francis Crick   less than   half |

......Rosalind Franklin... and Maurice Wilkins worked out that DNA has a helical structure

by directing beams of ....X - rays............... onto crystallised DNA and looking at the

patterns they made as they bounced off. James Watson and ......Fransis crick.......... used

these ideas, plus the fact that the amount of adenine + guanine is .equal to..................

the amount of thymine + cytosine, to make a model of the DNA molecule.

Top Tips: Your DNA controls what proteins your cells make — and they control everything the cells do. That's why the discovery of the structure of DNA was such a massive breakthrough in biology.

B2 Topic 1 — Genes and Enzymes

Protein Synthesis

Q1 Tick the boxes to show whether the following statements are **true** or **false**.

		True	False
a)	Genes are sections of DNA that code for specific proteins.	✓	
b)	Each amino acid is coded for by a set of four base pairs.	✓	
c)	The order of bases in a gene determines the order of amino acids.	✓	
d)	mRNA contains two strands, like DNA.		✓
e)	Translation takes place in the nucleus.		✓
f)	Amino acids join together to make polypeptides.		
g)	Each protein is made with a unique number and sequence of amino acids — this is what determines its shape and function.		

Q2 On the section of **DNA** shown:

```
A G G C T A G C C A A T C G C C G A A G C T C A
| | | | | | | | | | | | | | | | | | | | | | | |
T C C G A T C G G T T A G C G
```

a) Finish the lower sequence of bases.

b) Calculate how many amino acids are coded for by this section of DNA.

....

Q3 Genes can have **mutations** in them.

a) What are mutations?

....

b) Are mutations always harmful? Explain your answer.

....

Q4 **mRNA** is a messenger molecule used by the cell as a template for making **proteins**.

a) **i)** How is a molecule of mRNA formed from a molecule of DNA?

....

....

ii) Is this step called transcription or translation? ....

b) How do mRNA and ribosomes work together to build proteins?

....

....

....

....

Enzymes

Q1 a) Write a definition of the word 'enzyme'.

....

b) In the space below, draw a sketch to show how an enzyme's **shape** allows it to break substances down.

c) For an enzyme to work, the substrate must **fit exactly** into its active site. Give the name for this type of mechanism.

....

Q2 Draw lines to match the words below about **enzyme action** with their meanings.

active site   the chemical substance that an enzyme works on

specificity   the idea that enzymes only work with one substrate

substrate   the part of an enzyme which the substrate attaches to

Q3 **Enzymes** are involved in all sorts of reactions in the body, both **outside** and **inside cells**.

a) Name **one** type of reaction catalysed by enzymes that takes place **outside** cells.

....

b) Name **two** types of reaction catalysed by enzymes that take place **inside** cells.

....

Q4 Briefly describe how you could use **iodine solution** to measure the rate of an enzyme-controlled reaction.

....

....

....

6

More On Enzymes

Q1 Tick the correct boxes to show whether the sentences are **true** or **false**.

		True	False
a)	You can investigate the effect of temperature on enzymes by using different water baths.	✓	
b)	The rate of most chemical reactions can be increased by lowering the temperature.		✓
c)	Most cells are damaged at very high temperatures.	✓	
d)	Each enzyme has its own optimum temperature and pH, where it is most active.	✓	
e)	All enzymes work best at neutral pH.		✓

Q2 This graph shows the results from an investigation into the effect of **temperature** on the rate of an **enzyme** catalysed reaction.

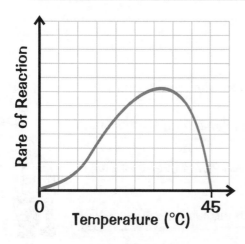

a) What is the **optimum** temperature for this enzyme?

...........32.5 °C................................

b) Describe what happens to the structure of an enzyme at temperatures **above** its optimum.

....The....active....site....becomes..........
....denatured...................................
....

Q3 The graph on the right shows how the **rate** of an enzyme-catalysed reaction is affected by **substrate concentration**.

a) Explain why the graph climbs steeply at first.

....because....the....rate....increases....
....as...the...enzyme...has...more.....
....substrates....to....catalyse...........

b) Explain why the graph levels off after point X.

....Because....the....amount....that the....Enzyme can....
....react....with...detec...........................
....

B2 Topic 1 — Genes and Enzymes

More On Enzymes

Q4   Stuart has a sample of an enzyme and he is trying to find out what its **optimum pH** is.
Stuart tests the enzyme by **timing** how long it takes to break down a substance at
different pH levels. The results of Stuart's experiment are shown below.

pH	Time taken for reaction (seconds)
2	101
4	83
6	17
8	76
10	99
12	102

a)   Draw a line graph of the results on the grid below.

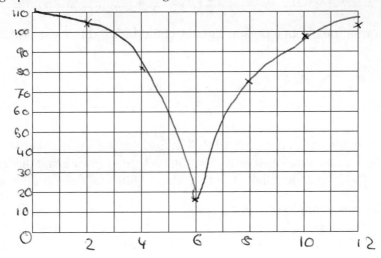

b)   Roughly what is the **optimum** pH for the enzyme?

...........6..

c)   Explain why the reaction is very slow at certain pH levels.

....

d)   Would you expect to find this enzyme in the stomach? Explain your answer.

no because the stomach is acidic..

e)   Describe two things that Stuart would need to do to make sure his experiment is a fair test.

1. ....

2. ....

Top Tips: Enzymes crop up a lot in Biology so it's worth spending plenty of time making sure
you know all the basics. If you're finding things a bit dull, you could always take a little break and eat
some tofu to make sure you have enough protein to make lots of delightful enzymes.

The Human Genome Project

Q1 Tick the boxes to show whether these statements about the **human genome** are **true** or **false**.

True False

a) The aim of the Human Genome Project was to find all of the 25 000 or so human genes. ☐ ☑

b) Thousands of scientists worldwide collaborated on the Human Genome Project. ☑ ☐

c) Scientists now know the function of every one of the human genes. ☑ ☐

Q2 The Human Genome Project could lead to big improvements in **medical treatment**.

a) Explain how information about a person's genes could be used to **prevent** diseases.

The gene that makes them susceptible to the diseeas could be replaced

b) Explain how information about a person's genes could be used to **treat** diseases.

....

....

Q3 Soon it may be possible to test a person's DNA to find out if they are likely to suffer from heart disease. Marco's genotype makes it likely that he will suffer from **heart disease** at an early age. Explain how it could have a **negative effect** on Marco if this fact was made available to:

a) an **employer** who was about to offer him a job.

They may not want to because of the risk

b) an **insurance company** who were about to give him life insurance.

It would inflat the price

c) Marco himself.

He may feel down and depressed

Q4 Police investigators can analyse DNA samples taken from the scene of a **crime** and compare this to the DNA of a **suspect**. In the future, it may be possible to look at the DNA samples from the crime scene and work out from them what the suspect **looks like**.

a) Underline any of the following characteristics that could be deduced from a person's DNA.

<u>i)</u> whether they have blue or brown eyes. ii) whether they have a scar on their cheek.

<u>iii)</u> whether they are male or female. iv) whether they are fat or thin.

b) Explain **why** some characteristics could be worked out from the DNA, but others could not.

some are genetic and some are caused by enviromental factors

Genetic Engineering

Q1   Fill in the gaps in the passage below to explain **how** genetic engineering is carried out.

> The useful ....*gene*............. is 'cut' out from one organism's chromosome
>
> using ....*Enzymes*........ . Enzymes are then used to cut another
>
> organism's chromosome and the useful ....*gene*............ is inserted.
>
> This technique produces ....*perfect*........... organisms.

Q2   Genetic engineering is used to produce **human insulin**.

a)   What type of organism is genetically modified to make human insulin?

.......*Bacteria*...

b)   Explain why producing insulin in this way can benefit humans.

.......*because human bodys can except it*...

....

Q3   **Golden Rice** was developed in order to increase the amount of **vitamin A** that could be obtained from a rice crop. It is estimated that a person would only have to eat **144 g** of Golden Rice per day in order to receive the recommended daily allowance of vitamin A, compared with **2.3 kg** of natural basmati rice.

a)   The new genes introduced into the Golden Rice plant make it produce a chemical that the humans body turns into vitamin A. Give the name of this chemical.

.....*Beta carotene*...

b)   Calculate how much **more** natural basmati rice you need to eat than Golden Rice to get your recommended daily allowance of vitamin A.

.......*2.156 kg*..

c)   It has been suggested that Golden Rice would be very useful as a crop in developing countries. Explain why it might be useful in such countries.

.......*Because rice is part of the diet there and*.............................
.......*vitamin A deficiency is a common problem*.............................
here

Top Tips: Before some clever-clogs worked out how to genetically modify organisms to make it, insulin for diabetics had to be extracted from animals and purified. Not easy, and not a nice thought for the diabetics either. So being able to make pure insulin in the lab was a real breakthrough.

B2 Topic 1 — Genes and Enzymes

Genetic Engineering

Q4 A crop plant had been genetically modified to make it **resistant to herbicides**. Some people were **concerned** that, as a result, wild grasses growing nearby might also become resistant to herbicides. Scientists decided to check whether this had happened.

The scientists sprayed herbicide onto 100 plants in an area next to the GM crop, and onto 100 plants from a second area far away from the GM crop.

Their results are shown in the table below.

Number of grass plants dying after spraying	
In area next to GM crop	In area far away from GM crop
83	85

a) Explain the reason for testing a group of plants that had not been growing near the GM crop.

to see if there was a difference

b) How could the scientists have made the results of this experiment **more reliable**?

They could have tested three of each type of area

c) The scientists decided that there was no significant difference between the two groups of plants. Explain whether you agree or disagree with this conclusion.

I agree because there is little difference from 85 to 83. The two that died could have been from other causes

d) If the scientists are right in their conclusion, does this prove that the concerns about genes for resistance spreading are unfounded? Explain your answer.

Yes

e) If wild grasses become resistant to herbicides, what **problems** might this cause?

They may grow and spread out of control

Mitosis

Q1 Tick the boxes to show whether the following statements are **true** or **false**.

		True	False
a)	Human body cells are diploid.	✓	☐
b)	There are 20 pairs of chromosomes in a human cheek cell.	☐	✓
c)	Chromosomes are found in the cytoplasm of a cell.	☐	✓
d)	Before a cell divides by mitosis, it duplicates its DNA.	✓	☐
e)	Mitosis is where a cell splits to create two genetically identical copies.	✓	☐
f)	Each new cell produced in mitosis gets one chromosome from each pair.	☐	✓
g)	Organisms use mitosis in order to grow.	✓	☐
h)	Organisms do not use mitosis to replace damaged cells.	☐	✓

Q2 The following diagram shows the different stages of **mitosis**.
Write a short description to explain each stage.

a) The chromosomes are duplicated

b) The chromosomes pair up

c) The poles of the cell direct the pairs

d) each new cell has the correct number of chromosomes

e) ....

Q3 Complete the following passage using the words below.

> runners   strawberry   variation   asexual   reproduce   genes

Some organisms use mitosis to .... For example, ...

plants produce .... this way, which become new plants. This is known

as .... reproduction. The offspring have exactly the same

.... as the parent, which means there's no genetic ....

Meiosis

Q1   Circle the correct word from each pair to complete the sentences below.

a)   Gametes are sex cells. During **asexual** / **sexual** reproduction two gametes combine to form a new cell that will grow into a new organism.

b)   Gametes are **diploid** / **haploid**. This means they have **one copy** / **two copies** of each chromosome. This is so that when two gametes combine the resulting cell has the right number of chromosomes.

c)   Human body cells have **23** / **46** chromosomes and human gametes have **23** / **46** chromosomes. When the gametes combine you get **23** / **46** chromosomes again.

Q2   Tick the boxes to show whether the following statements are **true** or **false**.

		True	False
a)	Meiosis halves the number of chromosomes.	☐	☐
b)	Meiosis forms gametes that are genetically identical.	☐	☐
c)	In humans, meiosis only happens in the reproductive organs.	☐	☐
d)	At fertilisation, two haploid gametes join to form a diploid zygote.	☐	☐

Q3   Draw lines to match each description of the stage of **meiosis** to the right diagram below.

a)

b)

c)

d)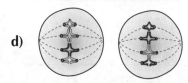

e)

The pairs are pulled apart, mixing up the mother and father's chromosomes into the new cells. This creates genetic variation.

Before the cell starts to divide it duplicates its DNA to produce an exact copy.

There are now 4 gametes, each containing half the original number of chromosomes.

For the first meiotic division the chromosomes line up in their pairs across the centre of the cell.

The chromosomes line up across the centre of the nucleus ready for the second division, and the two arms of each chromosome are pulled apart.

Top Tips: It's easy to get confused between **mitosis** and **meiosis**. Mitosis produces cells for growth and replaces damaged cells. Meiosis is for sexual reproduction and creates gametes.

Cloning Mammals

Q1 Complete each of the statements about **cloning** below by circling the correct words.

a) Cloning is a type of **asexual / sexual** reproduction.

b) Cloning produces cells with genes that are genetically **different from / identical to** the original cell.

Q2 Draw lines to match each of the 'cloning terms' below with its meaning.

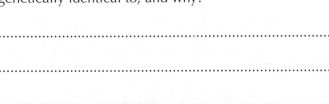

diploid nucleus   a developing fertilised egg

enucleation   body cell nucleus containing the full number of chromosomes

embryo   removal of the nucleus from a cell

Q3 The diagram shows the **procedure** that can be used to **clone** a sheep.

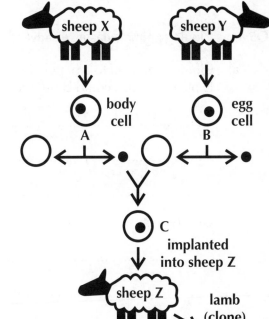

a) Which of the labelled cells in the diagram are genetically identical to each other? Explain your answer.

....

....

....

b) Which of the sheep (X, Y or Z) will the clone be genetically identical to, and why?

....

....

....

c) When the embryo stage is reached in this process, it is possible to divide up the embryo cells, and implant different cells into different surrogates. What would be the effect of doing this?

....

d) In normal sexual reproduction, fertilisation is the fusion of the female and male gametes and their genetic material. Explain the difference between this process and cloning.

....

....

....

B2 Topic 1 — Genes and Enzymes

14

<u>Cloning Mammals</u>

Q4   **Cloning** mammals has lots of practical uses.

a)   Scientists are creating genetically modified pigs, whose organs are compatible with the human body. Explain why being able to clone these pigs could benefit humans.

....

....

....

b)   Circle **two** other reasons why humans might want to clone mammals.

Cloning animals is easy and fast.

Cloning increases the genetic variety of a species.

Studying cloned animals could help us to understand the ageing process.

Cloning could be used to help preserve endangered species.

Q5   Cloning animals has its **disadvantages**.

a)   Cloning can lead to a population of animals having a reduced gene pool. Explain why this could cause problems for the animals.

....

....

....

b)   Give **two** other problems associated with cloning animals.

....

....

Q6   The first **mammal** to be cloned from an adult body cell was **Dolly the sheep**. She was born in 1996.

Describe how you could clone a mammal, starting with a body cell and an unfertilised egg cell.

....

....

....

....

....

B2 Topic 1 — Genes and Enzymes

Stem Cells

Q1   Tick the correct boxes to show whether the following statements are **true** or **false**.

		True	False
a)	Cells in an early embryo are unspecialised.	☐	☐
b)	Blood cells are undifferentiated.	☐	☐
c)	Nerve cells are specialised cells.	☐	☐
d)	Adult stem cells are as versatile as embryonic stem cells.	☐	☐
e)	Stem cells in bone marrow can differentiate into any type of cell.	☐	☐
f)	Most animal cells lose the ability to differentiate at an early stage.	☐	☐
g)	Lots of plant cells lose the ability to differentiate at an early stage.	☐	☐

Q2   Scientists in the UK are carrying out research into the use of stem cells in **medicine**.

a)   Describe one way in which stem cells are **already** used in medicine.

....

....

b)   Describe how it might be possible to use embryonic stem cells to treat disease in the future.

....

....

....

Q3   People have **different opinions** when it comes to embryonic **stem cell research**.

a)   Give one argument **in favour** of stem cell research.

....

....

b)   Give one argument **against** stem cell research.

....

....

Top Tips: In the future stem cells might be used to cure all sorts of diseases we can't cure now. But to get there we need to do research, and any research that uses embryos is going to be controversial. So it's a good idea to listen to all the arguments on both sides so you can work out what you think.

Mixed Questions — B2 Topic 1

Q1   Your **DNA** carries the **instructions** that tell your cells how to make **proteins**.

a)   The sequence of bases in part of one strand of a DNA molecule is as follows:

> A–A–T–C–C–A–A–T–C

Write down the **complementary sequence** of bases on the other strand of DNA.

....

b)   Name the **two people** who built the first accurate model of the structure of DNA.

....

c)   Complete each of the following statements about DNA by circling the correct words.

    i) A DNA molecule is made up of **two / three** strands of DNA coiled into a **double / triple** helix.

    ii) The strands are held together by **covalent bonds / hydrogen bonds** between pairs of bases.

    iii) Adenine always pairs with **thymine / cytosine** and guanine always pairs with **thymine / cytosine**.

d)   A mutation in a rabbit's gene caused one of its proteins to stop working properly.
Explain how a mutation can affect a protein's function like this.

....

....

....

Q2 a)   What unique characteristic do **stem cells** have which ordinary body cells don't have?

....

b)   Suggest why **embryos** contain many stem cells.

....

....

c)   Scientists have experimented with growing stem cells in different conditions.

    i) What is the name of the process by which stem cells **divide** for growth?

....

    ii) Complete this sentence about the process you named in part **i)** by circling the correct word.

> This process makes two cells that are genetically **identical / different** to the original cell.

Mixed Questions — B2 Topic 1

Q3 Mosquitoes have **three pairs** of **chromosomes** in their body cells. The diagram below shows a cell from a mosquito which is about to divide by **meiosis**.

a) Draw the chromosomes in one of the cells produced from this cell:

   i) after the first division stage of meiosis.   **ii)** after the second division stage of meiosis.

b) To draw the diagram, a scientist looked at the mosquito cell under a light microscope.
   The actual cell is **0.001 cm** wide. The image of the cell is **0.8 cm** wide.
   Calculate the magnification of the image.

   ....

   ....

Q4 **Proteins** are large molecules coded for by **DNA**.

a) Explain how each of the following are involved in building **new proteins**.

   i) Genes ....

   ii) Amino acids ....

   iii) Codons ....

   iv) mRNA ....

   v) Ribosomes ....

b) Some **human diseases** are caused by a **lack** of a **working protein**, e.g. people with type 1 diabetes don't produce enough of the protein insulin or don't produce any at all.
   Briefly describe how bacteria can be genetically modified to make human insulin.

   ....

   ....

   ....

B2 Topic 2 — Life Processes

Respiration

Q1 Part of the **word equation** for one type of **respiration** is shown below.

a) Complete the equation for respiration.

.... + oxygen → carbon dioxide + ... (+ ....)

b) What type of respiration is this? ....

Q2 Which of these statements is **not** true of respiration? Underline the correct answer.

It is a process used by all living organisms.　　It releases energy from food.

It is another word for breathing.　　It can be aerobic or anaerobic.

Q3 Give **three** things that the body uses the **energy** obtained in respiration for.

....

....

Q4 Draw lines to match the **body part** or **process** to the correct description.

capillaries	The system that provides the food source needed for respiration.
circulatory system	The movement of particles from areas of higher concentration to areas of lower concentration.
diffusion	The smallest blood vessels that carry blood to all body cells.
digestive system	The system that carries substances like glucose, oxygen and carbon dioxide around your body.

Q5 The diagram shows **blood** passing through **muscle tissue**.

a) On the diagram, draw labelled arrows to show whether **oxygen (O_2)**, **glucose (G)** and **carbon dioxide (CO_2)** move **into** or **out of** the muscle cells.

b) Explain how these substances move into and out of the blood in terms of concentration.

....

....

....

Respiration and Exercise

Q1 Humans can respire **aerobically** — if there isn't enough oxygen available we can also respire **anaerobically**.

a) Give **one** disadvantage of anaerobic respiration compared to aerobic respiration.

....

....

b) In what circumstances would a human start respiring anaerobically?

....

....

c) Write the **word equation** for anaerobic respiration in humans.

.... → .... (+ ....)

Q2 Joe investigated how **exercise** affects his **heart rate**. He took his **pulse** after **sitting still** for five minutes, after **walking** for five minutes and after **running** for five minutes. Joe's results are shown on the graph on the right.

a) How many beats per minute did running increase Joe's heart rate by, compared to sitting still?

....

b) Explain why running increases Joe's heart rate more than walking does.

....

....

....

....

c) Joe has a **stroke volume** of 65 cm³. Calculate Joe's **cardiac output**, in cm³ per minute, when he is **sitting still**.

cardiac output = heart rate × stroke volume

....

....

<u>*Respiration and Exercise*</u>

Q3　Jim is a keen runner. He takes part in a 400 metre race. The **graph** below shows Jim's **breathing rate** before, during and after the race.

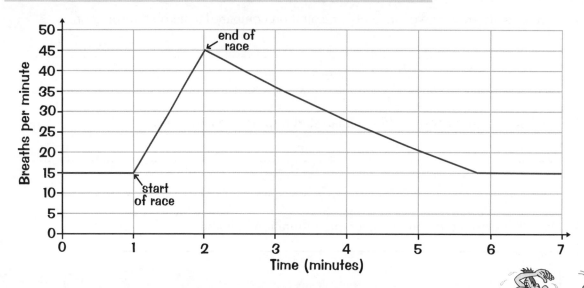

a)　How much does Jim's breathing rate go up during the race?

.... **breaths per minute**

b)　Explain why exercise makes Jim's breathing rate increase.

....

....

....

....

c)　As he gets to the end of the race, Jim's muscles start to hurt.
Explain why his muscles feel painful.

....

....

....

d)　Explain why Jim's breathing rate **doesn't** return to normal immediately after the race. Use the term '**EPOC**' in your answer.

EPOC stands for 'excess post-exercise oxygen consumption'.

....

....

....

....

Photosynthesis

Q1   Circle the correct word(s) in each pair to complete the passage below.

> Stomata are tiny holes found on the surface of the leaf that are
> used for **mineral uptake / gas exchange**. They allow carbon dioxide
> to diffuse **in / out** and oxygen to diffuse **in / out** of the leaf during
> photosynthesis. The stomata also allow water vapour to **leave / enter**
> the leaf — this water **loss / gain** is called **transcription / transpiration**.

Q2   **Photosynthesis** is the process that produces 'food' in plants. Use some of the words from the box below to complete the equation for photosynthesis.

oxygen	carbon dioxide	nitrogen	water	glucose	sodium chloride

.... + ... $\xrightarrow[\text{chlorophyll}]{\text{sunlight}}$ .... + ...

Q3   Tick the boxes to show whether the following statements are **true** or **false**.

True False

a) Photosynthesis happens inside the chloroplasts.

b) Photosynthesis happens in all plant cells.

c) Plants absorb carbon dioxide from the air.

d) Plant cells don't respire.

e) Sunlight provides the energy for photosynthesis.

Q4   Circle the most appropriate word(s) from each pair to complete the following statements.

a) The rate of photosynthesis depends on the availability of **raw materials / products**.

b) When photosynthesis is taking place **quickly / slowly**, more oxygen gas is being produced.

c) You can measure the rate of photosynthesis by counting the bubbles of **oxygen / carbon dioxide** produced by some pondweed in a given time.

Top Tips: Photosynthesis is one of those ideas that's absolutely central to biology. After all, if green plants couldn't trap the sun's energy, that would pretty much be the end of life on Earth — and certainly of us. So why not go and hug a tree now to say thanks. Or at least be kind to a pot plant...

Photosynthesis

Q5 A diagram of a leaf in cross-section is shown below.

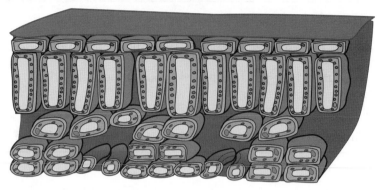

Suggest how each of the following features of the leaf are important for photosynthesis:

a) The leaf has a **broad surface**.

....

....

b) The leaf is **green**.

....

....

Q6 Below are some straightforward questions about **limiting factors**. Hooray.

a) Explain the meaning of the term "limiting factor".

....

b) List **three** things that can limit the rate of photosynthesis.

1. ....

2. ....

3. ....

c) The limiting factor at a particular time depends on the environmental conditions, e.g. season (such as winter). Name **two** other environmental conditions that may affect the rate of photosynthesis.

1. ....

2. ....

The Rate of Photosynthesis

Q1   Lucy investigated the **volume of oxygen** produced by pondweed at **different intensities of light**. Her results are shown in the table below.

bubbles of oxygen

pondweed

Relative light intensity	1	2	3	4	5
Vol. of O₂ produced in 10 mins (ml)	12	25	13	48	61

a)   Plot a graph of her results.

b)   i)   One of Lucy's results is probably wrong.
        Circle this point on the graph.

     ii)   Suggest what error Lucy might have made
           when she collected this result.

        ....

        ....

        ....

c)   Describe the relationship shown on the graph between light intensity and photosynthesis rate.

     ....

     ....

d)   Would you expect this relationship to continue if Lucy continued to increase the light intensity?
     Explain your answer.

     ....

     ....

Q2   Farmer Fred doesn't put his cows out during the winter because the grass is not growing.

a)   State **two** differences between summer and winter conditions
     that affect the rate of photosynthesis in the grass.

     1. ....

     2. ....

b)   How are the rate of photosynthesis and the growth rate of grass related?

     ....

     ....

The Rate of Photosynthesis

Q3   Seth investigated the effect of different concentrations of **carbon dioxide** on the rate of photosynthesis of his Swiss cheese plant. The results are shown on the graph below.

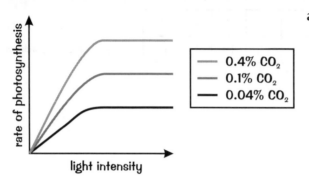

a)   What effect does increasing the concentration of CO_2 have on the rate of photosynthesis?

....

....

....

....

b)   Explain why all the graphs level off eventually.

....

....

Q4   Average **daytime summer temperatures** in different habitats around the world are shown in the table below.

Habitat	Temperature (°C)
Forest	19
Arctic	0
Desert	32
Grassland	22
Rainforest	27

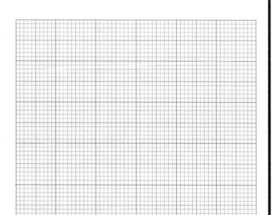

a)   Plot a **bar chart** for these results on the grid.

b)   From the values for temperature, in which area would you expect fewest plants to grow?

....

c)   Suggest a reason for your answer above using the terms **enzymes** and **photosynthesis**.

....

....

....

d)   **Explain** why very few plants can usually grow in the desert even though it has a much higher average temperature than the rainforest where many varieties of plants can grow.

....

....

Osmosis

Q1 This diagram shows a tank separated into two by a partially permeable membrane.

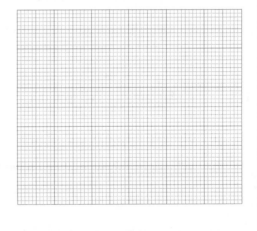

	Water molecule
	Sugar molecule

a) On which side of the membrane is there the higher concentration of water molecules?

....

b) In which direction would you expect **more** water molecules to travel — from A to B or from B to A?

....

c) Predict whether the level of liquid on side B will **rise** or **fall**. Explain your answer.

The liquid level on side B will ....**, because** ....

....

Q2 Some **potato cylinders** were placed in solutions of different **salt concentrations**. At the start of the experiment each cylinder was 50 mm long. Their final lengths are recorded in the table below.

Concentration of salt (molar)	Final length of potato cylinder (mm)	Change in length of potato cylinder (mm)
0	60	
0.25	58	
0.5	56	
0.75	70	
1	50	
1.25	45	

a) Plot the points for concentration of salt solution vs final length of potato cylinders on the grid.

b) Work out the change in length of each of the cylinders and complete the table above.

c) Study the pattern of the results.

   i) State the salt concentration(s) that produced unexpected results. ....

   ii) Suggest a method for deciding which of the results are correct.

   ....

d) State **three** factors that should have been kept constant to ensure this was a fair test.

....

....

26

Water Uptake and Loss in Plants

Q1 Flowering plants have **tube networks** for moving substances around.

a) Name the vessels that carry **sugars** around the plant. ....

b) Circle the correct word from each pair to complete the following sentence.

> Sugars are made in the **roots** / **leaves** and transported to parts of the plant that are **growing** / **dying** and to the plant's **storage** / **protective** tissues.

Q2 Choose from the following words to complete the passage.
Each word should only be used once, or not at all.

> | osmosis | leaves | evaporation | roots | flowers |
> | phloem | diffusion | transpiration | xylem |
>
> Most water leaves plants through the .... by the processes of
> .... and .... This creates a slight shortage
> of water in the leaf, which draws water from the rest of the plant through the
> .... vessels. This causes more water to be drawn up from
> the .... This whole process is called ....

Q3 A diagram of a **cell** found in the **root** of a **plant** is shown on the right.

a) Name the type of cell shown. ....

b) Why does this type of cell have the particular shape shown?

....

c) Explain why water moves into the plant's roots from the soil.

....

....

d) Explain how these specialised cells absorb mineral ions from the soil.
Use the words **active transport**, **concentration**, **respiration** and **energy** in your answer.

....

....

Top Tips: Water transport is the name of the game here — this stuff is all about how a plant keeps a steady stream of water moving from its roots, up its stem and into its leaves.

B2 Topic 2 — Life Processes

Distribution of Organisms

Q1 Tick the boxes to show whether the following statements are **true** or **false**.

	True	False

a) A habitat is the place where an organism lives. ☐ ☐

b) The distribution of an organism is how an organism interacts with its habitat. ☐ ☐

c) To study the distribution of an organism you can measure how common it is in two sample areas and compare them. ☐ ☐

Q2 Circle the correct word from each pair to complete the following statements.

a) You would use a pitfall trap to investigate the distribution of **ground insects** / **pond animals**.

b) The top of a pitfall trap is **completely covered** / **partly open**.

c) The sides of a pitfall trap are **steep** / **shallow** so that insects that fall into it **can** / **can't** get out again.

Q3 Sally sampled the population of **water snails** in two ponds.

a) Name a piece of equipment that Sally might have used to collect the snails.

....

b) Sally sampled each pond **three** times. The table below shows her results. Complete the table by filling in the missing numbers.

	Sample 1	Sample 2	Sample 3	Mean number of snails
Pond 1	2 snails	6 snails	7 snails	
Pond 2	10 snails	9 snails		11 snails

Q4 Mark wants to compare the distribution of beetles in two different areas. He decides to collect the beetles using a **pooter**.

a) Briefly describe how to collect an insect using a pooter.

....

....

b) Explain how Mark could use a pooter to compare the distribution of beetles in the two areas.

....

....

c) Name **two** things Mark needs to keep the same both times to make sure his test is fair.

1. ....   2. ....

More on the Distribution of Organisms

Q1 Environmental factors can affect how organisms are distributed.

a) **Light intensity** is an environmental factor. Name a device you could use to measure light intensity.

....

b) i) Name **one** other environmental factor that can affect the distribution of organisms.

....

ii) Name a piece of equipment that you could use to measure this factor.

....

Q2 Some students wanted to estimate the size of the population of **clover plants** around their school. To do this, they use the piece of equipment shown on the right.

a) What is this piece of equipment called?

....

b) The school field is 250 m long by 180 m wide. Hannah counted 11 clover plants in a 1 m² area of the field. **Approximately** how many clover plants are there likely to be on the whole field?

....

....

c) Lisa decided to collect data from five different 1 m² areas of the school field. Her results are shown in the table below.

	Area 1	Area 2	Area 3	Area 4	Area 5
No. of plants	11	9	8	9	7

i) What was the **average** number of clover plants per m² in Lisa's survey?

....

ii) Use Lisa's data to estimate the population size of clover plants on the field.

....

d) Whose estimation of population size is likely to be more accurate? Explain your answer.

....

....

Top Tips: Some questions may feel like you're doing maths rather than biology... but you can't get away from things like averages — you do need to know how to work them out for the exam. Booo.

Mixed Questions — B2 Topic 2

Q1 Humans can respire **aerobically** and **anaerobically**.

a) Give a definition of respiration, including where it happens in the body.

....

....

b) Complete the following sentences about anaerobic respiration in humans.

> Anaerobic respiration is respiration without ....
>
> A waste product, ..., is produced. ....
>
> energy is released during anaerobic respiration than during aerobic respiration.

c) Anaerobic respiration is not as efficient as aerobic respiration. Why is it still useful to us?

....

....

Q2 The diagram shows a **plant**, A, growing in a **tropical rainforest**.

plant A

a) Which factor is most likely to limit the rate of photosynthesis in plant A? Explain your answer.

....

....

b) Give **two** other factors that often limit the rate of photosynthesis in plants.

....

c) Plant A needs to take in water to keep photosynthesising.

i) Give the name of the vessels that carry water from the plant's roots to its leaves.

....

ii) Explain how the **transpiration stream** helps to keep the leaves supplied with water.

....

....

....

Mixed Questions — B2 Topic 2

Q3 A student was given **three solutions** labelled X, Y and Z. He set up the experiment shown on the right and left it for a day. At the end of the experiment, the water outside the membrane contained particles X and Y, but not Z.

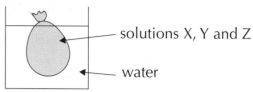

solutions X, Y and Z

water

a) Name the process by which particles of X and Y moved through the membrane.

....

b) What can you conclude about the relative sizes of the X, Y and Z particles?

....

c) X, Y and Z were solutions of amino acid, protein and glucose. Which of these solutions was Z?

....

d) During the experiment, some water particles moved from the beaker into the membrane. Name the process the water particles moved by. ....

Q4 Eve and Bill work together to study the **distribution** of **harebells** in a meadow. They each pick a **sample area** and use a **quadrat** to estimate the population size.

Harebells are pretty little blue flowers.

a) Define the term 'distribution'.

....

b) Explain how you can use a **1 m² quadrat** to find the **mean number** of harebells **per m²** in an area.

....

....

....

c) The results of Bill and Eve's investigation are shown in the table on the right.

	Number of harebells				
	Quadrat 1	Quadrat 2	Quadrat 3	Quadrat 4	Mean
Bill's area	5	7	2	4	
Eve's Area	8	11		12	10

i) Fill in the gaps in the results table.

ii) Eve has read that harebells grow best in **acidic soil**. She wonders if that's why there are more harebells in her area. Suggest how Eve could test this hypothesis.

....

....

d) Bill's friend Ben is studying the number of **spiders** in the meadow. The meadow is covered in **long grass**. Name a piece of equipment that Ben could use to collect spiders in the meadow.

....

Evidence For Evolution

Q1 Fossils were found in this sample of **rock**.

Fossil A
Fossil B

a) Explain what a fossil is.

....

....

b) Name **two** things that a fossil can tell us about an ancient organism.

1. ....

2. ....

c) Explain why scientists think that fossil B in the picture above is **older** than fossil A.

....

....

Q2 The fossil record is **incomplete** — there are gaps in it.
Give **three reasons** why we do not have fossils of some organisms.

1. ....

2. ....

3. ....

Q3 Tim is looking at the two pictures on the right. They show the **bones** in a **human hand** and a **bat's wing**.

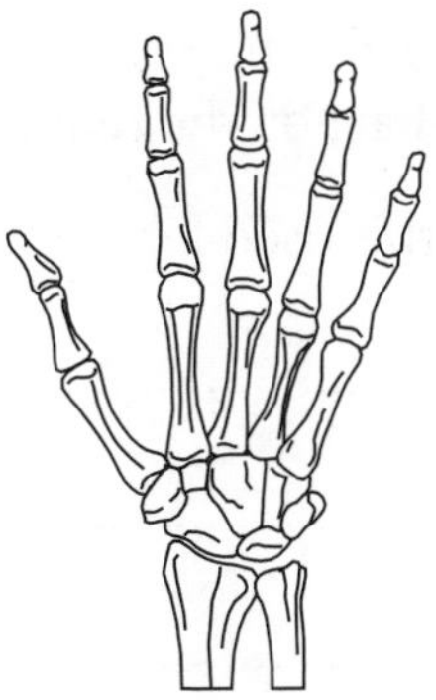

Human hand 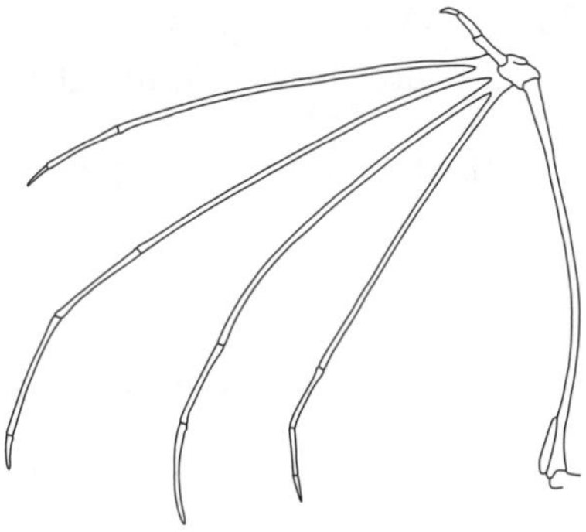   **Bat's wing**

a) Give the name for a limb that has **five digits**.

....

b) Tim says "Humans look quite different from bats, so I think they evolved from different ancestors." Is Tim likely to be correct? Explain your answer.

....

....

....

Growth and Development

Q1 If an organism increases in size or mass, it is **growing**.

a) Give **one** way to measure the **size** of an organism.

....

b) How do you measure the **dry mass** of an organism?

....

Q2 Animals and plants **grow** in different ways.

a) Draw lines to match each of the **growth processes** below to its correct definition.

CELL ELONGATION	When one cell splits into two by mitosis.
CELL DIFFERENTIATION	Where a cell expands, making the cell bigger.
CELL DIVISION	The process by which a cell changes to become specialised for its job.

b) Give **one** difference in growth between plants and animals.

....

....

Q3 A baby's growth was recorded. The results are shown on the **growth chart** on the right.

a) Explain what a growth chart is used for.

....

....

....

b) The baby's growth was above the 25th percentile at 6 months. Explain what the 25th percentile shows.

....

c) Would a doctor be concerned about the mass of this baby at 3 years? Explain your answer.

....

....

Cell Organisation and the Circulatory System

Q1 Complete the passage below using some of the words from the box.

function	tissue	organ	tissues	organs	cells	system	circulatory

A .... (e.g. muscle) is a group of similar .... that work

together to carry out a particular function. An .... (e.g. the heart) is a

group of different .... that work together to perform a particular function.

An organ system (e.g. the .... system) is a group of ....

working together to perform a particular function.

Q2 Sort the following list by writing each term in the correct place in the table below.

sperm   blood   digestive system   tree   liver
muscle   excretory system   white blood cell   leaf   cat

Cell	Tissue	Organ	Organ system	Organism

Q3 The diagram below shows the human **heart**, as seen from the front. The left atrium has been labelled for you. Complete the remaining labels **a)** to **h)**.

a) ....

b) ....

c) ....

d) ....

e) ....

f) ....

left atrium

g) ....

h) ....

Q4 Tick the boxes to say whether each statement below is **true** or **false**.

True False

a) Arteries always carry oxygenated blood. ☐ ☐

b) The atria of the heart have thicker walls than the ventricles. ☐ ☐

c) The right side of the heart pumps deoxygenated blood. ☐ ☐

d) Valves prevent blood flowing backwards. ☐ ☐

B2 Topic 3 — Organ Systems

The Circulatory System — The Blood

Q1   Which of these statements are **true** and which are **false**? Tick the correct boxes.

		True	False
a)	The main function of red blood cells is to fight germs.	☐	☐
b)	A higher than normal white blood cell count means you're more likely to get an infection.	☐	☐
c)	Glucose can be found in the blood.	☐	☐
d)	The liquid part of blood is called urea.	☐	☐
e)	Platelets seal wounds to prevent blood loss.	☐	☐

Q2   **Red blood cells** carry **oxygen** in the blood.

a)   i) Name the substance in these cells that combines with oxygen.   ....

  ii) Name the substance created when oxygen joins with this substance.   ....

b)   Red blood cells are replaced roughly every 120 days.
  Approximately how many times per year are all the red blood cells in the body replaced?

  ....

Q3   **White blood cells** defend the body against **disease**.

a)   State three ways in which white blood cells can protect your body from microorganisms.

  1. ....

  2. ....

  3. ....

b)   A man was feeling unwell and went to see his doctor. The doctor did a blood test and found that
  the patient's white blood cell count was higher than normal. Suggest a reason for this.

  ....

Q4   **Plasma** is the substance that carries everything in the blood.

a)   List **six** substances that are carried by **plasma**.

  ....

  ....

b)   For each of the substances listed in the table, state where in the body it is travelling **from** and **to**.

Substance	Travelling from	Travelling to
Urea		
Carbon dioxide		
Glucose		

The Circulatory System — Blood Vessels

Q1 Draw lines to match each of the words below with its correct description.

artery

capillary

lumen

vein

hole in the middle of a tube

microscopic blood vessel

vessel that takes blood towards the heart

vessel that takes blood away from the heart

Q2 Circle the correct word in each of the sentences below.

a) **Arteries / Veins** contain valves to prevent the blood going backwards.

b) **Capillaries / Veins** have walls that are permeable.

c) **Arteries / Capillaries** have smooth muscle in their walls.

d) The blood pressure in the **arteries / veins** is higher than in the **arteries / veins**.

Q3 Gareth did an experiment to compare the elasticity of **arteries** and **veins**. He dissected out an artery and a vein from a piece of fresh meat. He then took a 5 cm length of each vessel, hung different masses on it, and measured how much it stretched. His results are shown in the table.

a) Suggest **one** way that Gareth could tell which was the artery and which was the vein when he was dissecting the meat.

....

....

mass added (g)	length of blood vessel (mm)	
	artery	vein
0	50	50
5	51	53
10	53	56
15	55	59
20	56	-

b) If Gareth plots his results on a graph, which variable should he put on the vertical axis, and why?

....

c) Which vessel stretched more easily? Explain why this was.

....

d) Why did he take both vessels from the same piece of meat?

....

Top Tips: It really important to remember the differences between arteries, veins and capillaries — don't get them mixed up. It's the kind of thing that crops up on exams all the time...

The Digestive System and Enzymes

Q1   Fill in the boxes to label this diagram of the human **digestive system**.

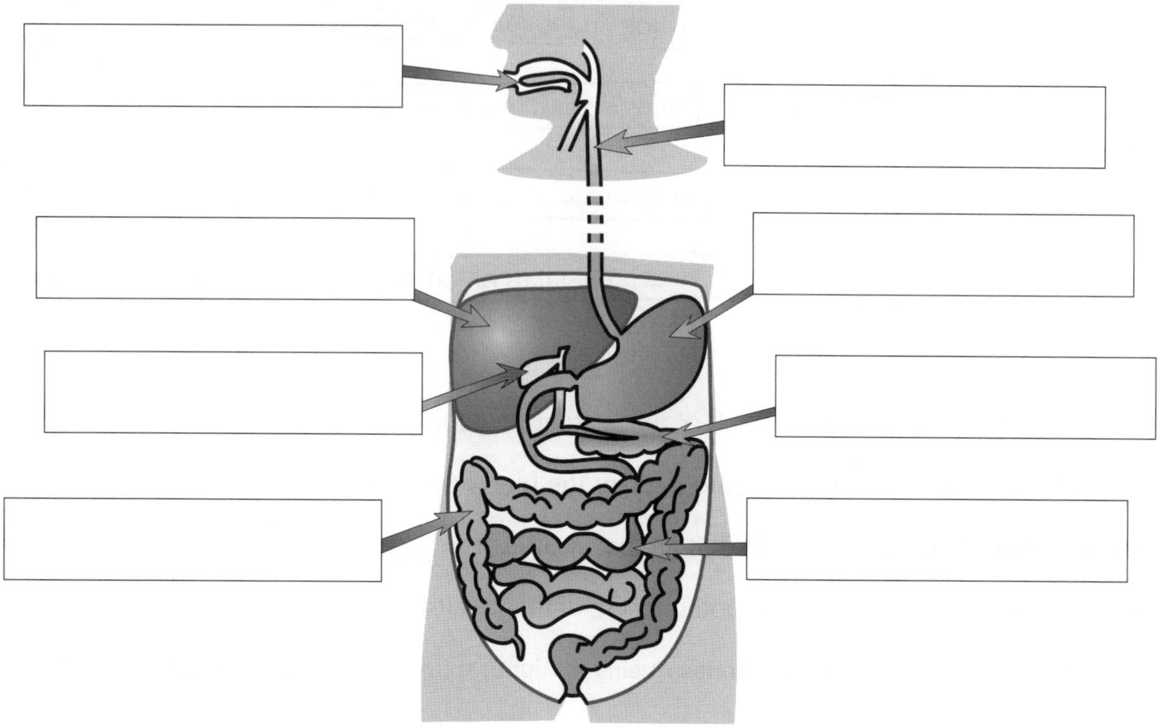

Q2   Number the boxes 1 to 4 to show the **order** that food passes through these parts of the **digestive system**.

☐ stomach

☐ mouth

☐ large intestine

☐ small intestine

Q3   During digestion, **enzymes** break **large molecules** down into **smaller molecules** that can be absorbed by the body.

a)   Look at the list below. **Underline** all the large molecules. **Circle** all the small molecules.

amino acids   sugars   proteins   fatty acids

fats   glycerol   starch

b)   Name one example of a **carbohydrase** enzyme. ....

c)   State what type of enzyme **pepsin** is. ....

B2 Topic 3 — Organ Systems

The Digestive System and Enzymes

Q4 Choose from the words below to complete the table showing where **amylase**, **protease**, **lipase** and **bile** are made. You may use some words more than once and you might not need some of them.

pancreas   liver   salivary glands   small intestine

large intestine   stomach   gall bladder   kidneys

Amylase	Protease	Lipase	Bile

Q5 Describe the **role** of each of the following in digestion:

a) Oesophagus ....

b) Gall bladder ....

c) Pancreas ....

d) Liver ....

e) Large intestine...

Q6 Fill in the boxes to show how the **three main food groups** are **broken down** during digestion.

a)

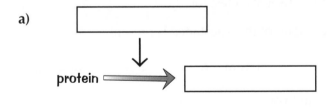

protein ⟶ [ ]

b)

lipase

[ ] ⟶ [ ] + [ ]

c)

[ ]

carbohydrate e.g. starch ⟶ [ ]

Top Tips: The stuff on digestion shouldn't take you too long to learn. The trickiest bits are probably all those enzyme names and what they do — so make sure you've got it all clear in your head.

Investigating Digestive Enzymes

Q1 Jenny investigated how the concentration of an enzyme affects the rate of digestion. She filled three pieces of visking tubing with **starch** solution and different concentrations of the enzyme **amylase**.

a) Explain why **visking tubing** is often used as a model for the gut.

....

....

b) Jenny put the pieces of visking tubing into three test tubes filled with distilled water, like this:

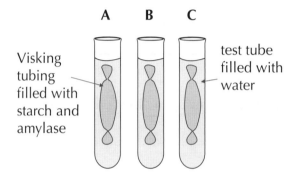

After four hours she tested the water outside each piece of tubing with Benedict's reagent. Her results are shown in the table below.

Tube	Amylase concentration	Colour of Benedict's reagent
A	5 mol/dm³	brick-red
B	0.5 mol/dm³	yellow
C	2 mol/dm³	orange

i) Name the substance that Benedict's reagent is used as a test for. ....

ii) State the colour of Benedict's reagent when none of this substance is present.

....

c) Explain what the results of Jenny's experiment tell you about how enzyme concentration affects the rate of reaction.

....

....

....

d) Jenny tried the experiment again using a very high concentration of amylase. This time the reaction didn't happen any faster than the reaction in tube A. Explain this result.

....

....

More on Digestion

Q1 a) Circle the correct words from each pair to complete this passage about **bile**.

> Bile is stored in the **gall bladder / pancreas** before being released into the **liver / small intestine**.
>
> Bile **acidifies / neutralises** the material from the stomach which provides the optimum pH
>
> for the **enzymes / microorganisms** in the rest of the digestive system to work. Bile breaks
>
> **fat / glycerol** into smaller droplets.

b) Explain how emulsification helps digestion.

....

....

Finest emulsion

Q2   **Peristalsis** helps the food that we eat get to the stomach from the mouth.

a) Explain what **peristalsis** is.

....

....

b) The diagram below shows peristalsis happening in the alimentary canal.

  i) Label the **longitudinal** muscles.

  ii) Label the **circular** muscles.

  iii) Add an arrow to the diagram to show which way the food is travelling.

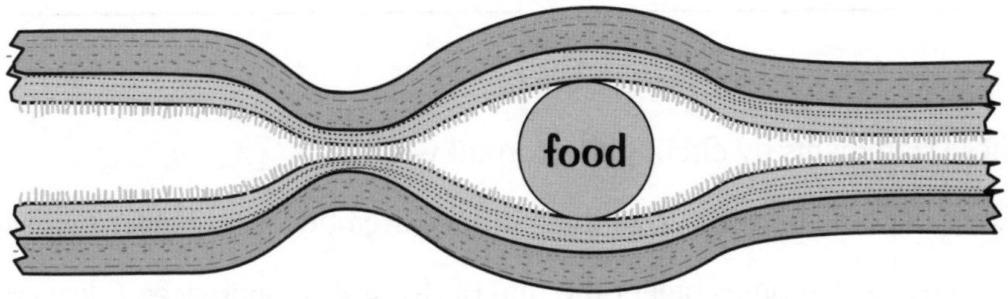

c) Briefly explain how peristalsis works.

....

....

....

More on Digestion

Q3   The inside of the **small intestine** is covered in millions of **villi**.

a)   Villi have a **single layer** of surface cells. Explain how this feature helps to speed up digestion.

    ....

b)   Give **one** other way that the villi are adapted to make digestion more efficient.
       Explain how the feature you have named helps to speed up digestion.

    Feature: ....

    Explanation: ....

    ....

Q4   Pablo conducted an experiment to investigate the effect of surface area on the uptake of nutrients, using four **gelatine cubes** of **different sizes**. He placed the cubes in a dish of food dye and measured how quickly they absorbed the dye.

Pablo's results are shown in the table below.

Size (cm)	Surface area (cm²)	Time taken for dye uptake (s)
1 x 1 x 1		41.6
2 x 2 x 2		9.3
5 x 5 x 5		1.7
10 x 10 x 10		0.4

a)   Calculate the missing values for **surface area**.

b)   Complete these statements by circling the correct word.

   i)   As the cubes become bigger in size their surface area becomes **bigger** / **smaller**.

   ii)   As the surface area becomes bigger the rate of dye uptake **increases** / **decreases**.

c)   Explain how the results from this experiment show that villi increase the rate of nutrient uptake from the gut.

    ....

    ....

    ....

Functional Foods

Q1 Explain what is meant by the term '**functional food**'.

....

....

Q2 **Probiotics** are added to some foods.

a) What are **probiotics**?

....

....

b) Name **one** example of a type of bacteria that is used in probiotic foods.

....

c) Circle **two** examples of common probiotic foods from the list below.

pasta

soya milk

yoghurts

vegetables

ham

Q3 Some people take **prebiotic** supplements.

a) What are **prebiotics**?

....

b) Suggest what health benefits a person might expect to get from taking a prebiotic supplement.

....

....

....

c) Give **two** natural sources of prebiotics.

1. ....

2. ....

Top Tips: Some bacteria are 'bad' and can cause disease but there are also 'good' bacteria. Everyone has 'good' bacteria in their guts — they're really important for digestion. Some functional foods are designed to try to help the 'good' bacteria to grow and thrive. How very kind of them...

Functional Foods

Q4   Two reports were published about eating **probiotic yoghurts**.

Report A was a magazine article published by the manufacturers of 'Well-U' probiotic yoghurt. It was about two ordinary women who ate two 'Well-U' yoghurts every day for a week.

Report B appeared in a journal. It was a study in which a trial group of 500 hospital patients were given a probiotic yoghurt for breakfast every day. A control group were given normal yoghurt.

Which of these reports has used a more reliable method for investigating probiotic yoghurts? Explain your answer.

....

....

....

Q5   Scientists did an experiment into the effectiveness of **stanol esters** in lowering people's **blood cholesterol**. They asked two groups of 100 people each to use a special spread instead of butter. Group A's spread was based on vegetable oil. Group B's spread was exactly the same, except that it contained large amounts of stanol esters. The cholesterol levels of each group were measured before the start of the experiment, and again after six months. The results are shown in the table.

	Group A / units	Group B / units
Mean blood cholesterol at start	6.3	6.4
Mean blood cholesterol after 6 mths	6.1	5.5

a)   Explain the purpose of Group A.

....

b)   Why did the scientists use 100 people in each group?

....

c)   What precautions should the scientists have taken when choosing people for this experiment, to make sure that their results were valid?

....

d)   Why is it necessary to measure the blood cholesterol before the experiment as well as at the end?

....

e)   Explain why it is important that people with high blood cholesterol take steps to lower it.

....

Mixed Questions — B2 Topic 3

Q1   **Growth** can involve cells **dividing**, **elongating** or **differentiating**.

   a)   Describe how plant growth differs from animal growth regarding:

   i) cell elongation ....

   ....

   ii) cell division ....

   ....

   iii) cell differentiation ....

   ....

   b)   Cells differentiate to become specialised cells, which form **tissues**. Describe what a **tissue** is.

   ....

   ....

Q2   The **blood** is a huge **transport system**.

   a)   **i)** Give the name of the blood cell shown on the right.

   ....

   ii) What is the function of this cell?

   ....

   b)   The cell on the right transports oxygen to all parts of the body.
   Give **two** ways in which this cell is adapted to perform its job.
   Briefly explain how each adaptation allows it to do its job well.

   ....

   ....

   ....

   c)   **Capillaries** carry the blood to cells, where oxygen and food can diffuse in, and waste substances
   can diffuse out. Explain how the capillaries are adapted to suit this function.

   ....

   ....

   ....

Mixed Questions — B2 Topic 3

Q3 The diagram shows part of the **circulatory system**.

a) Name the blood vessels labelled W, X, Y and Z.

W ....

X ....

Y ....

Z ....

Lungs

W →   ← Y

X →   ← Z

Body

b) State one difference in composition between
the blood entering the heart from the vena cava and the blood leaving the heart through the aorta.

....

c) Explain how the structure of an artery is adapted for its function.

....

....

d) i) Which type of blood vessel contains valves? ....

ii) What is the function of these valves?

....

Q4 During the **digestive process**, **fats** are broken down into fatty acids and glycerol.

a) Which enzyme is responsible for the digestion of fats?

....

b) **Bile** is also involved in the digestion of fats. Describe what bile does to fats.

....

c) i) Describe the roles that the **mouth** plays in the digestive process.

....

....

ii) Describe the roles that the **stomach** plays in the digestive process.

....

....

....

Atoms

Q1 Draw a diagram to show the structure of a **helium atom** in the box below. Label each type of **particle** on your diagram.

Helium has 2 of each type of particle.

Q2 **Complete** this table.

Particle	Mass	Charge
	1	+1
Neutron	1	
Electron		−1

Q3 **Complete** the following sentences by filling in the gaps or circling the correct options.

a) Atoms have a charge of ....

b) An atom has the same number of .... and ....

c) The nucleus is **huge** / **tiny** compared to the overall size of the atom.

Q4 What is it?

Choose from: **nucleus**   **proton**   **electron**   **neutron**

a) It's in the centre of the atom and contains protons and neutrons. ....

b) It moves around the nucleus in shells. ....

c) It's the lightest atomic particle. ....

d) It's heavy and has no charge. ....

<u>*Electron Shells*</u>

Q1 a) Tick the boxes to show whether each statement is **true** or **false**.

                                                                     True False

    i) Electrons orbit the nucleus in energy levels called shells. ☐ ☐

    ii) The highest energy levels are always filled first. ☐ ☐

    iii) The lowest energy levels are closest to the nucleus. ☐ ☐

    iv) Atoms are less likely to react when they have partially filled shells. ☐ ☐

    v) A maximum of eight electrons can occupy the first shell. ☐ ☐

b) Write out corrected versions of the **false** statements.

....

....

....

....

Q2 Identify **two** things that are wrong with this diagram.

1. ....

....

2. ....

....

Q3 Fill in the table with the **electronic configurations** for the following elements. The first one has been done for you.

Element	Electronic configuration
Beryllium	2.2
Oxygen	
Silicon	
Boron	
Aluminium	
Argon	

You'll need to use the periodic table (at the front of this book) to work out how many electrons each element has.

C2a Topic 1 — Atomic Structure and the Periodic Table

Electron Shells

Q4   **Chlorine** has 17 protons.

a)   What is its electronic configuration? ....

b)   Draw the electrons on the shells in the diagram.

c)   Why does chlorine react readily?

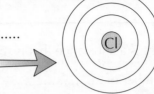

....

Q5   Draw the **full electronic configurations** for these elements. (The first three have been done for you.)

Hydrogen

Helium

Lithium

a) Carbon

b) Nitrogen

c) Fluorine

d) Sodium

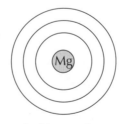

e) Magnesium

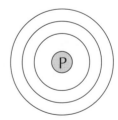

f) Phosphorus

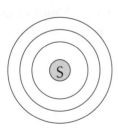

g) Sulfur

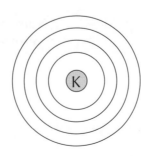

h) Potassium

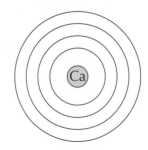

i) Calcium

Top Tips: Once you've learnt the 'electron shell rules' these are pretty easy — the first shell can only take two electrons, and the second and third shells a maximum of eight each. Don't forget it.

C2a Topic 1 — Atomic Structure and the Periodic Table

Elements

Q1 Fill in the blanks to complete the following passage about **elements** and **atoms**.

> An element is a substance that is made up from only one type of ....
>
> It's the number of .... in an atom that decides what element it is.
>
> The number of protons in an atom is called the .... number. The total
>
> number of protons and neutrons in an atom is called the .... number.

Q2 The diagrams below show four different substances. Circle those that contain only **one element**.

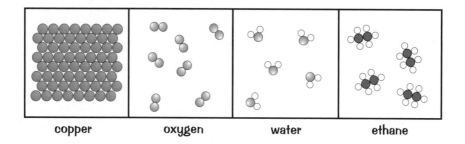

| copper | oxygen | water | ethane |

Q3 You are given the mass number and the atomic number of an element.

Explain how you would work out the number of neutrons the element has.

....

....

Q4 Fill in the table below, using the periodic table (at the front of this book) to help you.

Element	Symbol	Mass Number	Number of Protons	Number of Electrons	Number of Neutrons
Sodium	Na		11		
		16	8	8	8
Neon			10	10	10
	Ca			20	20

C2a Topic 1 — Atomic Structure and the Periodic Table

Isotopes and Relative Atomic Mass

Q1 Choose the correct words to **complete** this paragraph.

electrons	element	isotopes	protons	compound	neutrons

.... are different atomic forms of the same .... which have

the same number of .... but a different number of ....

Q2 Which of the following atoms are **isotopes** of each other? Explain your answer.

W $^{12}_{6}C$ **X** $^{40}_{18}Ar$ **Y** $^{14}_{6}C$ **Z** $^{40}_{20}Ca$

Answer .... and ....

Explanation ....

....

Q3 Draw lines to join the beginning of each sentence to its correct ending.

Relative atomic mass means

Relative abundance means

how much there is of each isotope compared to the total amount of the element in the world.

the average mass of the atoms of that element including the isotopes.

Q4 **Chlorine** has two main **isotopes**, ^{35}Cl and ^{37}Cl. Their relative abundances are shown in the table.

relative mass of isotope	relative abundance
35	3
37	1

Use this information to calculate the relative atomic mass of chlorine.

....

....

A Brief History of the Periodic Table

Q1   Fill in the gaps using the words provided to complete the following passage.

properties	reactivity series	table	atomic number

Mendeleev attempted to classify all known elements by arranging

them in a .... He used their

.... to do this.

Q2   Tick the boxes to show whether the following
statements about **Mendeleev** are **true** or **false**.

True False

a)   i) Mendeleev was able to predict the properties of undiscovered elements.   ☐ ☐

ii) Mendeleev put elements with similar properties in the same rows.   ☐ ☐

b)   Write out the corrected version of any **false** statements below.

....

....

Q3   Mendeleev left gaps in his table. He then predicted the discovery of an
element that would fill a gap in his Group 4, and called it '**ekasilicon**'.

a)   Explain why Mendeleev had to leave gaps in his table.

....

....

b)   The table below shows the **densities** of known elements in Mendeleev's Group 4.

'Ekasilicon' was eventually discovered and given another name.
Use the table to decide which of the elements below is ekasilicon.
Circle your choice.

Element	Density g/cm³
carbon	2.27
silicon	2.33
ekasilicon	
tin	7.31
lead	11.3

palladium, 12.0 g/cm³

beryllium, 1.85 g/cm³

germanium, 5.32 g/cm³

copper, 8.92 g/cm³

Top Tips: As new elements were discovered, Mendeleev's table grew to become the periodic
table we still use today. That makes him a bit of a legend in the wonderful world of chemists.

The Periodic Table

Q1 Choose from the words in the box to fill in the blanks in the sentences below.

> left   metals   vertical   right   similar   non-metals   horizontal   different

a) A period in the periodic table is a .... row of elements.

b) Most of the elements in the periodic table are ....

c) Non-metals are found on the .... side of the periodic table.

d) Elements in the same group have .... properties.

Q2 Tick the correct boxes to show whether the following statements are **true** or **false**.

          True False

a) Elements in a group have the same number of electrons in their outer shells. ☐ ☐

b) The periodic table shows the elements in order of descending atomic number. ☐ ☐

c) Each horizontal row in the periodic table contains elements with similar properties. ☐ ☐

d) The periodic table includes all the known compounds. ☐ ☐

Q3 **Argon** is an extremely unreactive gas. Use the periodic table to name two more elements that you would expect to have **similar properties** to argon.

1. ....   2. ....

Q4 Use a **periodic table** to help you answer the following questions.

a) Name one element in the same period as silicon. ....

b) Name one element in the same group as potassium. ....

c) Name one element that has 2 electrons in its outer shell. ....

Q5 **Fluorine** is a member of Group 7.

a) How many electrons does a fluorine atom have in its outer shell? ....

b) Explain why the only information you need to work this out is the group number.

....

Ionic Bonding

Q1 Choose the correct words from the list below to complete the passage.

elements	ionic	atoms	anions	compounds	cations

Atoms of different .... can form chemical bonds and join together

to create new .... One way they can do this is by ....

bonding. Electrons are transferred between atoms so they form ....

and ....

Q2 Tick one of the boxes below to show which statement is the best definition of an **ion**.

An ion is a compound that contains both positive and negative charges. ☐

An ion is a positively or negatively charged atom or group of atoms. ☐

An ion is a positively or negatively charged element. ☐

Q3 Tick the correct boxes to show whether the statements below are **true** or **false**.

		True	False
a)	In ionic bonding, ions lose or gain electrons to become atoms.	☐	☐
b)	Ions with opposite charges attract each other.	☐	☐
c)	Elements that lose electrons form positive ions.	☐	☐
d)	Elements that gain electrons form cations.	☐	☐
e)	Atoms form ions so that they can have full outer shells.	☐	☐

Q4 Use the **diagram** to answer the following questions.

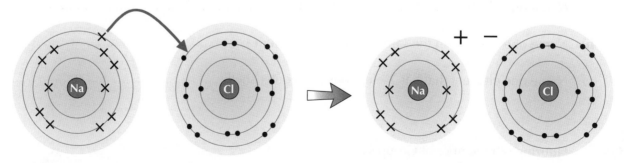

a) Which group of the periodic table does sodium belong to? ....

b) How many electrons does chlorine need to gain in order to have a full outer shell? ....

c) What is the charge on a sodium ion? ....

Ionic Bonding

Q5 Elements react in order to get a **full outer shell** of electrons.

a) How many electrons does magnesium need to **lose** to get a full outer shell? ....

b) How many electrons does oxygen need to **gain** to get a full outer shell? ....

c) Draw a 'dot and cross' diagram in the space provided to show what happens to the outer shells of electrons when magnesium and oxygen react.

> The diagrams in question 4 on the previous page are 'dot and cross' diagrams.

Q6 Atoms can **gain** or **lose** electrons to get a full outer shell.

a) How many electrons do the following elements need to **lose** in order to get a **full outer shell**?

   i) Lithium ....   **ii)** Calcium ....   **iii)** Potassium ....

b) How many electrons do the following elements need to **gain** in order to get a **full outer shell**?

   i) Oxygen ....   **ii)** Chlorine ....   **iii)** Fluorine ....

Q7 **Beryllium** is in **Group 2** of the periodic table.
Complete the following sentences by circling the correct word from each pair.

a) An atom of beryllium has **two** / **six** electrons in its outer shell.

b) It will form an ion by **gaining** / **losing** electrons.

c) The charge on a beryllium ion will be 2^+ / 2^-.

d) A beryllium ion is **an anion** / **a cation**.

e) Beryllium **can** / **can't** form ionic bonds with elements from Group 1.

f) Beryllium **can** / **can't** form ionic bonds with elements from Group 6.

Ionic Compounds

Q1 Use a 'dot and cross' diagram to show what happens to the outer shells of electrons when **sodium** and **oxygen** react to give **sodium oxide**.

Q2 Explain how sodium and chlorine atoms react to form the ionic compound **sodium chloride**.

....

....

Q3 Use 'dot and cross' diagrams showing the outer shells of electrons to explain why potassium chloride has the formula **KCl** but magnesium chloride has the formula **MgCl$_2$**.

Ionic Compounds

Q4   **Sodium chloride** is an ionic compound.

a)   Circle the statement from the list below that **best** describes the **structure** of sodium chloride.

> A regular lattice arrangement.   A cube.   A chain of positive and negative ions.

b)   Circle the correct words to explain why sodium chloride has a **high melting point**.

> Sodium chloride has very **strong** / **weak** electrostatic forces of attraction between
>
> the **negative** / **positive** sodium ions and the **negative** / **positive** chloride ions.
>
> This means that it needs a **small** / **large** amount of energy to break the bonds.

Q5   Mike carries out an experiment to find out if **magnesium oxide** conducts electricity.
He tests the compound when it's solid, when it's dissolved in water and when it's molten.

a)   Complete the following table of results.

	Conducts electricity? (Yes / No)
When solid	
When dissolved in water	
When molten	

b)   Explain your answers to part **a)**.

....

....

....

Q6   The melting point of **calcium chloride** is **772 °C** and that of **carbon chloride** is **−23 °C**.

Which one is an ionic compound? Explain your choice.

....

....

....

Top Tips: Ionic bonds are a bit of a one-trick pony — they always produce compounds with a
similar structure. So, once you've learnt that structure you can apply it to any ionic compound.

Naming Compounds and Finding Formulas

Q1 The names of compounds can tell us what **elements** they contain.

a) Use options from the box below to complete the passage about naming compounds.

oxygen	-IDE	hydrogen	-ATE	two	one	-ADE

When .... elements combine the compound's name is

'something ....'. When three or more different elements

combine and one of them is .... the compound's name is

'something ....'.

b) i) Which elements are present in potassium nitrate?

....

ii) Which elements are present in calcium carbonate?

....

Q2 Here are some elements and the **ions** they form:

> Make sure the charges on the ions balance.

beryllium, Be^{2+}   **potassium, K$^+$**   **iodine, I$^-$**   **sulfur, S^{2-}**

Write down the formulas of four compounds which can be made using these elements.

1. ....   3. ....

2. ....   4. ....

Q3 Give the **formulas** of the following ionic compounds. Use the table on the right to help.

a) potassium bromide ....

b) iron(II) chloride ....

c) calcium fluoride ....

d) sodium carbonate ....

e) iron(III) sulfate ....

Positive Ions		Negative Ions	
Sodium	Na$^+$	Chloride	Cl$^-$
Potassium	K$^+$	Fluoride	F$^-$
Calcium	Ca^{2+}	Bromide	Br$^-$
Iron(II)	Fe^{2+}	Carbonate	CO$_3^{2-}$
Iron(III)	Fe^{3+}	Sulfate	SO$_4^{2-}$

Q4 The formula of calcium nitrate is **Ca(NO$_3$)$_2$**.

The charge on the calcium ion is 2+. State the charge on the nitrate ion. ....

Preparing Insoluble Salts

Q1 A, B and C are symbol equations for reactions in which **salts** are formed.

   A $CuO(s) + H_2SO_4(aq) \rightarrow CuSO_4(aq) + H_2O(l)$

   B $2NaOH(aq) + H_2SO_4(aq) \rightarrow Na_2SO_4(aq) + 2H_2O(l)$

   C $Pb(NO_3)_2(aq) + H_2SO_4(aq) \rightarrow PbSO_4(s) + 2HNO_3(aq)$

Which equation (A, B or C) shows the formation of an insoluble salt by a precipitation reaction?

....

Q2 **Silver chloride** is an insoluble salt which is formed as a **precipitate** when silver nitrate and sodium chloride solutions are mixed together.

a) Complete the word equation for the reaction.

.... + ... $\rightarrow$ silver chloride + ...

b) After mixing the solutions to produce a precipitate, what further steps are needed to produce a dry sample of silver chloride?

....

....

....

Q3 Some salts are **soluble**.

a) Complete the table to show whether the following salts are soluble or insoluble in water.

Salt	Soluble	Salt	Soluble
copper nitrate	✓	calcium chloride	
lead nitrate		calcium nitrate	
sodium carbonate		lead sulfate	
copper carbonate	✗	sodium sulfate	

b) i) Lead nitrate and sodium sulfate are reacted together in solution. Name the two salts made in this reaction.

....

ii) Explain what you would see during this reaction.

....

....

....

Barium Meal and Flame Tests

Q1 Choose from the words below to complete the passage about barium sulfate.

bloodstream	toxic	insoluble	meal	soluble
blockages	invisible	gut	drink	opaque

Although barium salts are ...., barium sulfate can be

safely drunk because it is .... This means that it passes

through the body without being absorbed into the ....

Barium sulfate is .... to X-rays so it can be used to show

up a patient's .... This means that any problems

e.g. .... can be seen. Drinking barium before an X-ray

is known as a barium ....

Q2 **Flame tests** are often carried out to identify unknown substances.

a) Describe how you would carry out a flame test using a wire loop on an unknown powder.

....

....

b) Why would the results of this test be unreliable if the wire loop had not been cleaned properly?

....

Q3 Les had four samples of **metal compounds**. He carried out a flame test on each one.

a) Draw lines to match each of Les's observations to the metal cation producing the coloured flame.

brick-red flame	Na^+
yellow/orange flame	Cu^{2+}
blue-green flame	K^+
lilac flame	Ca^{2+}

b) Les wants to make a firework which will explode in his local football team's colour, **lilac**. Which of the following compounds should he use? Circle your answer.

silver nitrate   sodium chloride   barium sulfate

potassium nitrate   calcium carbonate

Testing for Negative Ions and Spectroscopy

Q1 Choose from the words given to complete the passage below.

carbon dioxide	limewater	acid	sodium hydroxide	hydrogen

Reacting an unidentified substance with dilute .... is a way of testing

for carbonate ions. If they are present then .... will be formed.

You can test for this by bubbling it through .... to see if it becomes milky.

Q2 Answer the following questions on testing for **sulfate** ions.

a) Which two **chemicals** are used to test for sulfate ions?

....

b) What would you **see** after adding these chemicals to a sulfate compound?

....

Q3 Deirdre wants to find out if a soluble compound contains **chloride** ions. Explain how she could do this.

....

....

....

Q4 Complete the following equations for **tests for negative ions**.

a) $Ag^+_{(aq)}$ + ... → $AgCl_{(s)}$

b) $2HCl_{(aq)}$ + $Na_2CO_{3(s)}$ → $2NaCl_{(aq)}$ + ...$_{(l)}$ + ...$_{(g)}$

c) .... + ... → $BaSO_{4(s)}$

You're being a bit negative today, aren't you?

No...

Q5 Spectroscopy is an **analytical technique** used in laboratories.

a) Name two elements that were discovered using spectroscopy.

1. .... 2. ....

b) Give one advantage of using spectroscopy to identify elements.

....

Covalent Bonding

Q1   Indicate whether each statement is **true** or **false**.

                                                                                            True False

    a)   Covalent bonding involves sharing one or more pairs of electrons.   ☐ ☐

    b)   Atoms react to gain a full outer shell of electrons.   ☐ ☐

    c)   When atoms make covalent bonds they form molecules.   ☐ ☐

    d)   Hydrogen can form two covalent bonds.   ☐ ☐

    e)   Carbon can form four covalent bonds.   ☐ ☐

Q2   **Complete** the following table to show how many electrons are needed to **fill up** the **outer shell** of these atoms.

Atom	Carbon	Chlorine	Hydrogen	Nitrogen	Oxygen
Number of electrons needed to fill outer shell					

Q3   Complete the following diagrams by adding the **electrons**. Only the outer shells are shown.

    a)   Hydrogen chloride (HCl)

    d)   Carbon dioxide (CO_2)

    b)   Oxygen (O_2)

    e)   Methane (CH_4)

    c)   Water (H_2O)

Q4   Why do some atoms **share** electrons?

    ....

    ....

Covalent Substances — Two Kinds

Q1 Fill in the blanks in the following paragraph by choosing words from the list.

weak	hard	small	easy	large	strong

Simple molecular covalent substances are made from .... molecules.

The covalent bonds that hold the atoms together are .... but the forces

between the molecules are quite .... Because of this it is fairly

.... to separate the molecules.

Q2 Complete the following sentences by circling the correct option, and explain your answers.

a) The melting and boiling points of simple molecular covalent substances are **low** / **high**.

....

b) Simple molecular covalent substances **conduct** / **don't conduct** electricity.

....

Q3 Circle the correct words to complete the following paragraph.

Giant molecular covalent structures contain **charged ions** / **uncharged atoms**. The covalent bonds

between the atoms are **strong** / **weak**. Giant molecular covalent structures have **high** / **low** melting

points and they are usually **soluble** / **insoluble** in water.

Q4 **Graphite** and **diamond** are both made entirely from **carbon**, but have different properties.

a) Explain why graphite's structure makes it a good material for making electrodes.

....

....

b) Explain how diamond's structure makes it useful for use in drill tips.

....

....

c) Explain why graphite's structure makes it a good lubricant, but diamond's structure doesn't.

....

....

Classifying Elements and Compounds

Q1 Complete the following table by placing a **tick** or a **cross** in each box.

Property	Ionic Lattice	Giant Molecular	Simple Molecular
High melting and boiling points			
Can conduct electricity when solid		except graphite	
Can conduct electricity when molten		except graphite	

Q2 The table gives data for some **physical properties** of a selection of elements and compounds.

substance	state at room temp	melting point / °C	boiling point / °C	electrical conductivity	
				solid	liquid
A	solid	114	184	poor	poor
B	gas	-73	-10	poor	poor
C	solid	3550	4827	poor	poor
D	solid	858	1505	poor	good
E	solid	1495	2870	good	good
F	liquid	0	50	poor	poor

a) **i)** Identify one substance that is **likely** to have a **simple molecular** structure. ....

ii) Explain your answer.

....

....

....

b) **i)** Which of the substances is **most likely** to have a **giant molecular** structure? ....

ii) Explain your answer.

....

....

....

Top Tips: Chemists spend a lot of time identifying substances. Hiding behind those safety goggles there's a frustrated detective trying to get out. Anyway, the bottom line is that you need to be able to work out whether a substance is an ionic lattice, giant molecular or simple molecular. The clues are boiling point, melting point and electrical conductivity. Go get 'em Sherlock.

Separation Techniques

Q1 Some liquid mixtures are **immiscible** and some are **miscible**.

a) Draw lines to match the type of mixture to its description and separation method.

description

| Separates out into layers when allowed to stand |

| Doesn't separate out into layers when allowed to stand |

type of mixture

Miscible

Immiscible

separation method

Fractional distillation

Separating funnel

b) A mixture of two liquids, A and B, is separated using a **separating funnel**.
Liquid B is denser than liquid A.

Which liquid, A or B, would be removed **first** when the tap on the funnel is opened?

....

Q2 Air is a source of **chemicals** that can be used in industry.

a) Put numbers in the boxes to show the order of the stages in the fractional distillation of air.

☐ Air is filtered to remove dust.

☐ Air is cooled to -200 °C.

☐ Liquefied air enters the fractionating column and is heated slowly.

☐ Carbon dioxide freezes and is removed. Water vapour condenses and is removed.

b) Fill in the gaps with the words below to explain why air can be separated by fractional distillation.

compound	boiling points	vapour	mixture	weights

Air is a .... of gases with different ....

c) Name two gases that are obtained when air is separated by fractional distillation.

1. ....

2. ....

<u>Chromatography</u>

Q1 Ella is using **paper chromatography** to compare the **ink** used on a **threatening letter** with the ink found in three **suspects' printers**.

a) Briefly outline the method Ella will use.

....

....

....

b) Using words from the list below, complete the following passage to describe how paper chromatography works.

chromatogram	solvent	lines	filter	graph	ink	spots

The .... seeps up the paper taking the samples of inks with it.

The different chemicals in the inks form separate .... on the

paper. This result is called a ....

c) The results Ella gets when she analyses the ink from the threatening letter and the ink from the suspects' printers are on the right. Which suspect(s) can she **exclude** from the investigation?

....

Ink on letter   Ink from suspect 1   Ink from suspect 2   Ink from suspect 3

Q2 A **food colouring** was analysed using **paper chromatography**. The chromatogram shown below was produced.

Use the formula to work out the R_f value of each dye.

$$R_f = \frac{\text{distance travelled by substance}}{\text{distance travelled by solvent}}$$

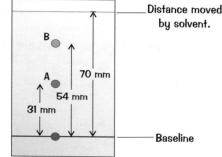

Distance moved by solvent.

B   A   70 mm   54 mm   31 mm   Baseline

a) Dye A ....

b) Dye B ....

C2a Topic 3 — Covalent Compounds and Separation Techniques

Mixed Questions — C2a Topics 1, 2 & 3

Q1   **Iodine** exists as simple **covalent molecules**, I_2.

a)   Explain why iodine has a low melting point.

....

....

b)   Predict whether iodine is likely to be able to conduct electricity. Justify your prediction.

....

....

Q2   **Diamond** and **graphite** both contain only carbon atoms.

Explain why graphite and diamond have very **high melting points**.

....

....

Q3   **Calcium** is a reactive metal in **Group 2** of the periodic table.

a)   Give the electronic configuration of a calcium **atom**.

....

b)   i) Based on its position in the periodic table, name an element
which has similar properties to calcium.

....

ii) Explain your answer.

....

c)   Calcium reacts with **chlorine** to form an ionic compound. The charge on the chloride ion is 1−.

i) Write the word equation for this reaction.

....

ii) Write the symbol equation for the reaction.

....

Mixed Questions — C2a Topics 1, 2 & 3

Q4 Answer the following questions about the **periodic table**.

a) If an element is in Group 1, how many electrons will it have in its outer electron shell? ....

b) An ion of an element has a 2+ charge. Which group is the element **most likely** to be in? ....

c) If an ion has a 1– charge, then which group is it **most likely** to be in? ....

You can use the periodic table (at the front of this book) to help you.

d) Complete this table by filling in the **electronic configurations** of the elements:

Period	Group 1		Group 2	Group 3	Group 7	Group 0	
2	Li	2,1	Be	B	F	Ne	
3	Na		Mg	Al	Cl	Ar	2.8.8

Q5 Hydrogen atoms can exist as three **isotopes** — ^{1}**H** (hydrogen), ^{2}**H** (deuterium) and ^{3}**H** (tritium).

a) What is an isotope?

....

....

b) Explain why the relative atomic mass of an element isn't always a whole number.

....

....

c) Complete the table.

isotope	number of protons	number of neutrons	number of electrons
^{1}H			
^{2}H			
^{3}H			

d) The atomic number is often left out of the isotope symbol.
For instance, it is acceptable to write ^{12}**C** for carbon-12 rather than $^{12}_{6}$**C**.

i) Define the term **atomic number**.

....

ii) Explain why the atomic number can be left out of the isotope symbol.

....

....

Mixed Questions — C2a Topics 1, 2 & 3

Q6   Stanley is trying to identify a mystery substance.

First he dips a clean wire loop in the substance and puts it in a Bunsen flame.

a)   What result would you expect Stanley to see if the mystery compound contained Ca^{2+} ions?

....

...and add a splash of $CaSO_4$, with a dollop of $MgBr_2$ and a dash of Worcester sauce...

b)   In fact, he sees a blue-green flame. What can Stanley conclude?

....

c)   Stanley suspects that his compound is a sulfate. Describe a test he could do to see if he's right.

....

....

d)   Stanley does the test for a sulfate, and sees a white precipitate form in the solution.

   i) Write down an **ionic equation** for the formation of this white precipitate. Include state symbols.

   ....

   ii) Write down the formula of Stanley's mystery compound. ....

Q7   **Lithium** is a metallic element in **Group 1** of the periodic table.

a)   Draw a diagram to show the electronic configuration in a lithium atom.

Use the periodic table to help you.

b)   **Fluorine** is in **Group 7** of the periodic table. Its electronic configuration is shown below.

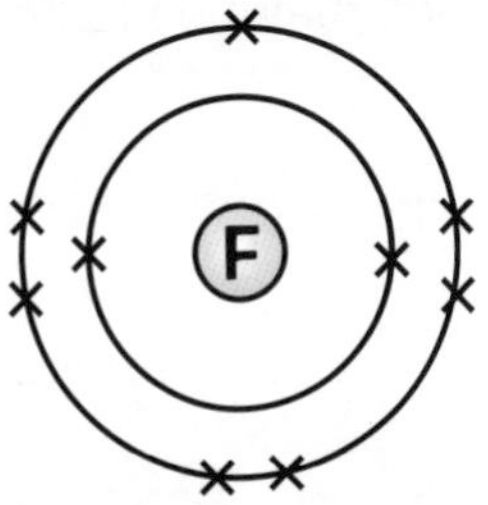

   i) Give the chemical formula for the compound that forms between lithium and fluorine.

   ....

   ii) What type of bonding is involved in this compound? ....

Properties of Metals

Q1 Most **metals** that are used to make everyday objects are found in the **central section** of the periodic table.

a) What name is given to this group of metals?

....

b) What property of a typical metal from this group would make it suitable for electrical wires?

....

c) Give one property of compounds formed by these metals.

....

Q2 All metals have a similar **structure**. This explains why many of them have similar **properties**.

a) Draw a labelled diagram showing the structure of a typical metal.

Think about the reason why metals are good conductors.

b) What is unusual about the electrons in a metal?

....

Q3 Imagine that a space probe has brought a sample of a new element back from Mars. Scientists think that the element is a **metal**, but they aren't certain. Give **three properties** they could look for to provide evidence that the element is a **metal**.

1. ....

2. ....

3. ....

Top Tips: Remember, most elements are metals and most metals have similar properties. This is because all metals have a similar structure. But don't go thinking that they're all identical — there are lots of little differences which make them useful for different things.

Group 1 — The Alkali Metals

Q1 **Sodium**, **potassium** and **lithium** are all alkali metals.

a) Highlight the location of the alkali metals
on this periodic table.

b) State two physical properties of alkali metals.

1. ....

2. ....

c) Put sodium, potassium and lithium in order of increasing reactivity with water.

least reactive   ....

....

most reactive   ....

d) Explain why the alkali metals become more reactive as their atomic number increases.

....

....

....

Q2 Three different **alkali metals**, A, B and C,
were dropped into bowls of water. The time
taken for each piece to **vanish** was recorded
and is shown in the table.

METAL	TIME TAKEN TO VANISH (s)
A	27
B	8
C	42

a) i) Which of these is the most reactive metal?
How can you tell?

....

....

ii) The three metals used were lithium, sodium and potassium.
Use the results shown in the table to match them up to the correct letters A, B and C.

A = ...   B = ...   C = ...

b) i) What products would be formed in a reaction between sodium and water?

....

ii) "The amount of time taken for rubidium to vanish in water will be shorter than metal A,
but longer than metal B". Is this statement correct? Explain your answer.

....

....

<u>Group 1 — The Alkali Metals</u>

Q3 Complete the passage using some of the words from the box below.

two	potassium	one	oxygen	hydroxide	hydrogen	carbonate

Potassium is a soft metal with .... electron(s) in its outer shell.

It reacts vigorously with water, producing ....

and .... gas.

Q4 A piece of **lithium** was put into a beaker of water.

a) Write a word equation for the reaction that occurs.

....

b) Write a balanced symbol equation for the reaction that occurs.

....

c) Circle the word in the list below that describes the solution formed at the end of the reaction.

acidic   neutral   alkaline

Q5 **Caesium** and **francium** are alkali metals.

a) i) Look at the periodic table. Which metal would you expect to be more reactive?

....

ii) Explain your answer.

....

....

b) Both caesium and francium must be stored in oil. Suggest why this is.

....

....

> **<u>Top Tips:</u>** Make sure that when it comes to your exam, you're all clued up on the alkali metals. You need to know where they are in the periodic table, and what goes on in their reactions with water. Make sure you know about how their reactivity changes as you go down the group too.

C2b Topic 4 — Groups in the Periodic Table

Group 7 — The Halogens

Q1 Highlight the location of the halogens in this periodic table.

Q2 Draw lines to match the halogens to their **descriptions** and **reactivity**.

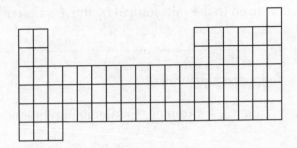

HALOGEN	DESCRIPTION	REACTIVITY
bromine	green gas	most reactive
chlorine	grey solid	least reactive
iodine	orange liquid	quite reactive

Q3 Tick the correct boxes to say whether these statements are **true** or **false**.

            True False

a) Chlorine gas is made up of molecules which each contain three chlorine atoms. ☐ ☐

b) Chlorine reacts with potassium to form an ionic compound. ☐ ☐

c) The halogens become less reactive as you go down the group. ☐ ☐

d) The halogens can lose electrons to form halide ions. ☐ ☐

e) When a more reactive halogen reacts with a solution containing halide ions and pushes out the less reactive halogen, this reaction is called a precipitation reaction. ☐ ☐

Q4 Halogens react with hydrogen to form **hydrogen halides**.

a) State the name of the compound formed when chlorine reacts with hydrogen.

....

b) The product of the reaction between chlorine and hydrogen is dissolved in water. Is the solution acidic or alkaline?

....

Group 7 — The Halogens

Q5 Halogens can react with **metals** to form salts.

a) What is the general name given to the salts formed by the reaction of a halogen with a metal?

....

b) Fill in the blanks in the following equations.

i) .... + bromine → aluminium bromide

ii) Potassium + ... → potassium iodide

iii) Magnesium + fluorine → ....

c) Write balanced symbol equations for each of the reactions in part **b)**, using the formulas given in the box below.

Mg	Br_2	KI	Al	$AlBr_3$	K	F_2	I_2	MgF_2

i) ....

ii) ....

iii) ....

Q6 Equal volumes of **bromine water** were added to three test tubes, each containing a different **halogen salt solution**. The results are shown in the table.

SOLUTION	RESULT
potassium chloride	no reaction
potassium bromide	no reaction
potassium iodide	reaction

a) Explain why there was no reaction when bromine water was added to potassium chloride solution.

....

....

b) Explain why there was a reaction when bromine water was added to potassium iodide solution.

....

....

....

c) Write a symbol equation for the reaction which took place in the potassium iodide solution when bromine water was added.

....

Group 0 — The Noble Gases

Q1   Where are the noble gases located in the periodic table?

....

Q2   Complete the table using the numbers provided to show trends in the **boiling points** and **densities** of the noble gases.

0.0018

-246

-186

0.0002

Element	Boiling point (°C)	Density (g/cm³)
Helium	-269	
Neon		0.0009
Argon		

Q3   The noble gases were **discovered** long after many of the other elements.

a)   Why did it take scientists so long to discover the noble gases?

....

....

b)   Circle the correct words to complete the passage below.

The noble gases were eventually discovered when scientists noticed that the density

of nitrogen made in **chemical reactions / fractional distillation** was different to the density

of nitrogen taken from **water / air** . They suggested that the nitrogen from the **water / air**

must have other **metals / gases** mixed in with it. Scientists used **fractional distillation /**

displacement reactions to separate the noble gases from the nitrogen.

c)   Explain why the noble gases are unreactive.

....

....

....

Top Tips: The examiners will expect you to know quite a bit about certain groups in the periodic table — the halogens, the alkali metals, the noble gases and the transition metals. Make sure you're clear on their general properties and how these change as you move down or up each group.

74

Energy Transfer in Reactions

Q1 Chemical reactions may be **exothermic** or **endothermic**.

a) Circle the correct words in this paragraph about **exothermic** reactions.

Exothermic reactions **take in** / **give out** energy overall, in the form of **heat** / **sound**. This is shown by a **fall** / **rise** in **temperature** / **mass**.

b) Tick the correct boxes to indicate whether the following reactions are exothermic or endothermic.

	Exothermic	Endothermic
i) Photosynthesis	☐	☐
ii) Combustion	☐	☐
iii) An explosion	☐	☐
iv) Dissolving ammonium nitrate in water	☐	☐

Q2 Fill in the missing words in this paragraph about **endothermic** reactions to make it correct.

Endothermic reactions .... energy overall from the surroundings in the form of .... This is often shown by a .... in ....

Q3 State whether bond **breaking** and bond **forming** are exothermic or endothermic reactions, and explain why in both cases.

Bond breaking ....

....

Bond forming ....

....

Q4 During the following reaction the reaction mixture's temperature **increases**.

$$AB + C \longrightarrow AC + B$$

a) Is the reaction exothermic or endothermic?

....

b) Which bond is stronger, A–B or A–C? Explain your answer.

....

Energy Transfer in Reactions

Q5   When **methane** burns in oxygen it forms carbon dioxide and water.
The bonds in the methane and oxygen molecules **break** and new bonds
are formed to make carbon dioxide and water molecules.

a)   Is energy taken in or given out when the bonds in the methane and oxygen molecules break?

....

b)   Is energy taken in or given out when the bonds in the carbon dioxide and water molecules form?

....

c)   Methane is a fuel commonly used in cooking and heating. Do you think that burning methane is
an exothermic or an endothermic process? Explain your answer.

....

....

d)   Which of the following statements about burning methane is true? Circle one letter.

A   The energy involved in breaking bonds is greater than the energy involved in forming bonds.

B   The energy involved in breaking bonds is less than the energy involved in forming bonds.

C   The energy involved in breaking bonds is the same as the energy involved in forming bonds.

Q6   Here are some practical uses of chemical reactions. Decide whether each reaction is
endothermic or **exothermic**. In the box, put **N** for endothermic and **X** for exothermic.

a)   A camping stove burns methylated spirit to heat a pan of beans. ☐

b)   Special chemical cool packs are used by athletes to treat injuries. ☐
They are placed on the skin and draw heat away from the injury.

c)   Self-heating cans of coffee contain chemicals in the base. When the ☐
chemicals are combined they produce heat which warms the can.

d)   Cooking fried eggs and bacon for breakfast. ☐

This is different to part **a)** — think about what
happens to the eggs and bacon while they're cooking.

Energy Changes and Measuring Temperature

Q1 The **energy level diagrams** below represent the energy changes in five chemical reactions.

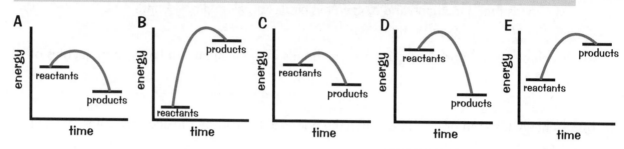

Write the letter of the diagram or diagrams that show: *The graphs are all to the same scale.*

a) an exothermic reaction? ....   **c)** the reaction that gives out the most energy? ....

b) an endothermic reaction? ....   **d)** the biggest energy change overall? ....

Q2 Fiz investigated the **temperature change** during a reaction. She added sodium hydroxide solution to dilute hydrochloric acid. She **measured the temperature** of the reaction over the first **30 seconds**.

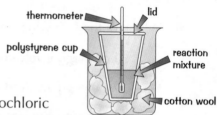

a) Fiz set up the equipment for the experiment as shown.

  i) Explain why Fiz should measure the temperature of the hydrochloric acid and sodium hydroxide before carrying out the reaction.

    ....

  ii) State the purpose of the lid and cotton wool used in the experiment.

    ....

    ....

  iii) Why is it difficult to get **an accurate result** for the temperature change in an experiment like this?

    ....

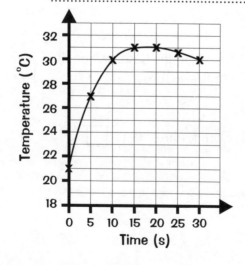

b) Fiz plotted her results on the graph shown.

  i) What was the increase in temperature due to the reaction?

    ....

  ii) Circle the words below that correctly describe the reaction in this experiment.

      neutralisation   **displacement**

    endothermic   **precipitation**   **exothermic**

Rates of Reaction

Q1 Circle the correct words to complete the statements below about **rates of reaction**.

a) The **higher** / **lower** the temperature, the faster the rate of a reaction.

b) A **higher** / **lower** concentration will reduce the rate of a reaction.

c) A smaller surface area of a solid reactant **increases** / **decreases** the rate of a reaction.

d) A catalyst **does** / **does not** affect the rate of a reaction.

Q2 Marble chips with **different surface areas** were reacted with excess hydrochloric acid. The **same mass** of marble was used each time. The graph below shows the amount of **gas** evolved when using large marble chips (X), medium marble chips (Y) and small marble chips (Z).

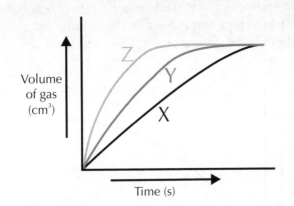

a) i) Which curve (X, Y or Z) shows the **fastest** reaction? Circle the correct answer.

        X   **Y**   **Z**

ii) How can you tell this by looking at the graph?

....

....

....

b) Why do all the reactions produce the **same** volume of gas?

....

c) On the graph, draw the curve you would expect to see if you used **more** of the marble chips with the largest surface area. Assume that all the other conditions are the same as before.

Q3 Another experiment investigated the **change in mass** during a reaction in which a **gas** was given off. The graph below shows the results for three experiments carried out under different conditions.

a) Suggest **why** reaction R involved a greater change in mass than reactions P and Q.

....

....

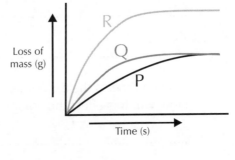

b) What might have caused the difference between reaction P and reaction Q?

....

....

Rates of Reaction Experiments

Q1   Choose from the words below to complete the paragraph.

surface area	slower	react	decrease	faster	increase

When you crush up a large solid into powder, you .... its surface

area. This means it reacts .... Large lumps have a smaller

.... , so they .... more slowly.

Q2   Matilda conducted an experiment to investigate the effect of **surface area** on rate of reaction.
She added dilute hydrochloric acid to **large marble chips** and measured the volume of gas
produced at regular time intervals. She repeated the experiment using the same mass of
powdered marble. Below is a graph of her results.

a) Which curve, A or B, was
obtained when **large pieces**
of marble were used?

....

b) On the graph opposite, draw the
curve you would get if you used
the **same mass** of **medium** sized
marble pieces. Label it C.

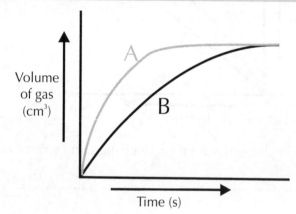

c) Balance the symbol equation for this reaction:

$$CaCO_3 + \quad HCl \rightarrow \quad CaCl_2 + \quad CO_2 + \quad H_2O$$

d) Is there enough information given above for you to be sure whether this was a **fair test** or not?
Explain your answer.

....

....

....

e) Matilda repeats the experiment using a greater mass of powdered marble.
How will this effect the volume of gas produced by the experiment?

....

Top Tips: The experiment on this page looks at the effect of surface area on the rate of a
reaction. But the same experiment can be used to measure any of the other factors that affect the rate.

Rates of Reaction Experiments

Q3   Sam did an experiment where marble chips were added to **highly concentrated** hydrochloric acid. He measured the **loss in mass** during the experiment. He did the experiment twice using the same conditions and then calculated averages for the results.

a)   Why did Sam do the experiment **twice** and calculate averages for the results?

....

b)   Sam did a second experiment in identical conditions but using a **lower concentration** of hydrochloric acid. The results of two runs are shown in the table below.

Time (s)	Run 1 — loss in mass (g)	Run 2 — loss in mass (g)	Average loss in mass (g)
5	1.1	0.9	
10	1.6	1.8	
15	2.7	2.3	
20	3.4	2.8	
25	3.6	3.4	
30	3.6	3.4	

i)   Fill in the last column of the table by calculating the **average loss in mass** for the two experiments.

ii)   The results of Sam's first experiment using highly concentrated of hydrochloric acid are shown below. Using the data you calculated in part **b) i)**, plot a line onto the graph showing the average loss in mass when Sam used a low concentration of hydrochloric acid.

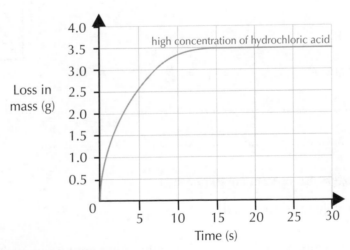

c)   **Circle** the letter(s) to show the **valid conclusion(s)** you might draw from this graph.

    A   Rate of reaction depends on the temperature of the reactants.

    B   Increasing the concentration of the acid has no effect on the rate of reaction.

    C   Rate of reaction depends on the acid concentration.

    D   Rate of reaction depends on the mass of the marble chips.

Rates of Reaction Experiments and Catalysts

Q1 Yasmin investigates the effect of **temperature** on the rate of the reaction between sodium thiosulfate and hydrochloric acid. When they react, a precipitate is formed and the mixture becomes **cloudy**. She mixes the reactants together in a flask and times how long a cross placed under the flask takes to disappear.

Here are some results from her investigation:

Temperature (°C)	20	30	40	50	60
Time taken for cross to disappear (s)	201	177		112	82

a) As the temperature increases, does the reaction get **faster** or **slower**? ....

b) One of the values in the table is missing. Circle the most likely value for it from the list below.

145 s   **192 s**   **115 s**

Q2 The decomposition of hydrogen peroxide can be used to investigate the effect of a **catalyst** on the rate of reaction. A student compared three different catalysts to see which was the most effective (increased the rate of reaction the most). Below is a graph of his results.

a) Explain what a catalyst is and what it does.

....

....

b) **i)** The student finds that manganese (IV) oxide is the most effective catalyst for this reaction. Using the graph, decide which curve (R, S, or T) represents the reaction using manganese (IV) oxide. Circle the correct letter.

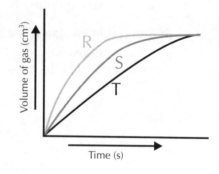

R   **S**   **T**

ii) Explain your answer.

....

....

Q3 **Catalytic converters** are used in car exhausts.

a) Describe what catalytic converters do.

....

....

b) Give two features of catalytic converters that make them well-suited to this role.

1. ....

2. ....

Collision Theory

Q1   Circle the correct words to complete the sentences.

a)   In order for a reaction to occur, the particles must **remain still** / **collide**.

b)   If you heat up a reaction mixture, you give the particles more **energy** / **surface area**.

c)   This makes them move **faster** / **more slowly** and so there is **more** / **less** chance of successful collisions.

d)   So, increasing the temperature increases the **concentration** / **rate** of reaction.

Q2   Draw lines to match up the **changes** with their **effects**.

increasing the temperature	provides a surface for particles to stick to and lowers the energy required by the particles to react
decreasing the concentration	makes the particles move faster, so they collide more often
adding a catalyst	gives particles a bigger area of solid reactant to react with
increasing the surface area	means fewer particles of reactant are present, so fewer collisions occur

Q3   The **concentration** of a solution may affect the rate of a reaction.

a)   i)   If you increase the concentration of reactants, does the rate of reaction **increase** or **decrease**?

....

ii) Explain your answer.

....

....

b)   In the boxes on the right complete the two diagrams —
one showing particles in a solution with a low concentration,
the other showing particles in a highly concentrated solution.

solvent particles   low concentration   high concentration

Q4   Here are four statements about **surface area** and **rates of reaction**.
Tick the appropriate boxes to show whether they are true or false.

		True	False
a)	Breaking a larger solid into smaller pieces decreases its surface area.	☐	☐
b)	A larger surface area means a faster rate of reaction.	☐	☐
c)	A larger surface area decreases the number of useful collisions.	☐	☐
d)	Powdered marble has a larger surface area than an equal mass of marble chips has.	☐	☐

Relative Formula Mass

Q1 What are the **relative atomic masses (A$_r$)** of the following:

a) magnesium ....

b) neon ....

c) oxygen ....

d) hydrogen ....

e) C ....

f) Cu ....

g) K ....

h) Ca ....

i) Cl ....

Q2 **Identify** the **elements** A, B and C.

Element A is ....

Element B is ....

Element C is ....

Element A has an A$_r$ of 4.
Element B has an A$_r$ 3 times that of element A.
Element C has an A$_r$ 4 times that of element A.

Q3 a) Explain how the **relative formula mass** of a **compound** is calculated.

....

b) What are the **relative formula masses (M$_r$)** of the following:

i) water (H_2O) ....

ii) calcium chloride ($CaCl_2$) ....

iii) potassium hydroxide (KOH) ....

iv) nitric acid (HNO_3) ....

v) sulfuric acid (H_2SO_4) ....

vi) ammonium nitrate (NH_4NO_3) ....

vii) aluminium sulfate ($Al_2(SO_4)_3$) ....

Q4 The equation below shows a reaction between an element, X, and water. The total M$_r$ of the products is **114**. What is substance X?

$$2X + 2H_2O \rightarrow 2XOH + H_2$$

....

....

Top Tips: The periodic table really comes in useful here. There's no way you'll be able to answer these questions without one (unless you've memorised all the elements' relative atomic masses — and that would just be silly). And luckily for you, there's one in the front of this book.

Two Formula Mass Calculations

Q1 a) Write down the **formula** for calculating the **percentage mass** of an element in a compound.

b) Calculate the percentage mass of the following elements in ammonium nitrate, NH_4NO_3.

i) Nitrogen ....

ii) Hydrogen ....

iii) Oxygen ....

Q2 **Nitrogen monoxide**, NO, reacts with oxygen, O_2, to form **oxide R**.

a) Calculate the percentage mass of nitrogen in **nitrogen monoxide**.

....

b) A 100 g sample of oxide R contains **30.4 g** of **nitrogen** and **69.6 g** of **oxygen**.
Work out the empirical formula of oxide R.

....

....

....

Q3 **31.9 g** of **aluminium** reacts with **288.1 g** of **bromine** to form a compound.
Work out the empirical formula of the compound.

....

....

....

Q4 a) Calculate the percentage mass of **oxygen** in each of the following compounds.

    A Fe_2O_3 **B** H_2O **C** $CaCO_3$

b) Which compound has the **greatest** percentage mass of oxygen? ....

<u>Calculating Masses in Reactions</u>

Q1 Anna burns **10 g** of **magnesium** in air to produce **magnesium oxide** (MgO).

a) Write out the **balanced equation** for this reaction.

....

b) Calculate the mass of **magnesium oxide** that's produced.

....

....

....

Q2 What mass of **sodium** is needed to make **2 g** of **sodium oxide**? $4Na + O_2 \rightarrow 2Na_2O$

....

....

....

Q3 **Aluminium** and **iron oxide** (Fe_2O_3) react together to produce **aluminium oxide** (Al_2O_3) and **iron**.

a) Write out the **balanced equation** for this reaction.

....

b) What **mass** of iron is produced from **20 g** of iron oxide?

....

....

....

Q4 When heated, **limestone** ($CaCO_3$) decomposes to form **calcium oxide** (CaO) and **carbon dioxide**.

How many **kilograms** of limestone are needed to make **100 kilograms** of **calcium oxide**?

The calculation is the same — just use 'kg' instead of 'g'.

....

....

....

....

C2b Topic 6 — Quantitative Chemistry

Calculating Masses in Reactions

Q5 **Iron oxide** is reduced to **iron** inside a blast furnace using carbon. There are **three** stages involved.

Stage A	$C + O_2 \rightarrow CO_2$
Stage B	$CO_2 + C \rightarrow 2CO$
Stage C	$3CO + Fe_2O_3 \rightarrow 2Fe + 3CO_2$

a) If **10 g** of **carbon** are used in stage B, and all the carbon monoxide produced gets used in stage C, what **mass** of CO_2 is produced in **stage C**?

Work out the mass of CO at the end of stage B first.

....

....

....

....

b) Suggest what happens to the CO_2 produced in stage C.

Look at where CO_2 is used.

....

Q6 **Sodium sulfate** (Na_2SO_4) is made by reacting **sodium hydroxide** (NaOH) with **sulfuric acid** (H_2SO_4). **Water** is also produced.

a) Write out the **balanced equation** for this reaction.

....

b) What mass of **sodium hydroxide** is needed to make **75 g** of **sodium sulfate**?

....

....

....

....

c) What mass of **water** is formed when **50 g** of **sulfuric acid** reacts with sodium hydroxide?

....

....

....

....

Top Tips: Masses, equations, formulas — they can all seem a bit scary. But don't worry, practice makes perfect. And once you get the hang of them you'll wonder what all the fuss was about.

C2b Topic 6 — Quantitative Chemistry

Percentage Yield

Q1 James wanted to produce **silver chloride** (AgCl). He added a carefully measured mass of silver nitrate to an excess of dilute hydrochloric acid. **1.2 g** of silver chloride was produced.

a) Explain what is meant by the **yield** of a chemical reaction.

....

b) i) Write down the formula for calculating the **percentage yield** of a reaction.

....

ii) James calculated that he should get 2.7 g of silver chloride. What was the **percentage yield**?

....

Q2 Aaliya and Natasha mixed together barium chloride ($BaCl_2$) and sodium sulfate (Na_2SO_4) in a beaker to produce barium sulfate. They **filtered** the solution to obtain the solid barium sulfate, and then transferred the barium sulfate to a clean piece of **filter paper** and left it to dry.

a) Aaliya calculated that they should produce a yield of **15 g** of barium sulfate. However, after completing the experiment they found they had only obtained **6 g**.

Calculate the **percentage yield** for this reaction.

....

b) Suggest two reasons why their actual yield was lower than their theoretical yield.

1. ....

....

2. ....

....

Q3 The reaction between magnesium and oxygen produces a white powder, **magnesium oxide**. Four samples of magnesium, each weighing 2 g, were burned and the oxide produced was weighed. The **expected** yield was **3.33 g**.

Sample	Mass of oxide (g)
A	3.00
B	3.18
C	3.05
D	3.15

a) What is the percentage yield for each sample?

....

....

....

b) Which of the following are possible reasons why the yield was not 100%? Circle their letters.

A Some of the oxide was lost before it was weighed   **B** Too much magnesium was burned

C Not all of the magnesium was burned   **D** The reaction was too fast

Percentage Yield

Q4 Complete the table of results showing the **percentage yields** from different experiments.

You can use the space below for working out.

Actual yield	Theoretical yield	Percentage yield
3.4 g	4.0 g	a)
6.4 g	7.2 g	b)
3.6 g	c)	80%
d)	6.5 g	90%

Q5 Fill in the gaps to complete the passage below using the words from the box.

waste	expensive	yield	harmful	speed	environment	commercially

Chemical reactions can produce lots of unwanted .... products.

These can be .... and may pose a threat to the ....

It can be .... to dispose of these products safely. Chemists look to

find reactions that give a high percentage .... , produce

.... useful products and take place at a suitable ....

Q6 Limestone consists of **calcium carbonate**. If calcium carbonate is heated it leaves solid **calcium oxide**. When **100 tonnes** of limestone were heated, **42 tonnes** of calcium oxide were produced.

a) Write the equation for this reaction. ....

Use a periodic table to help you with this question.

b) What was the theoretical yield?

....

....

c) Using your answer from part **b)**, calculate the percentage yield.

....

d) Why are you unlikely ever to get a 100% yield from this process?

....

....

88

Mixed Questions — C2b Topics 4, 5 & 6

Q1 The results of a reaction between **calcium carbonate** and **hydrochloric acid** are shown on the graph.

a) The products of this reaction are calcium chloride (which forms a colourless solution), water and carbon dioxide. Suggest how the rate of this reaction could be measured.

....

....

b) Which part of the curve shows the fastest rate of reaction — A, B or C? ....

c) Explain what happens to the reaction at point C.

....

d) i) At 35 °C, the reaction followed the curve shown on the graph. Draw two other complete curves on the same diagram to show how the rate of reaction might change at 25 °C and 45 °C.

ii) Explain why raising the temperature affects the rate of reaction.

....

....

e) Give three factors other than temperature that affect the rate of reaction.

....

Q2 **Iodine** vapour reacts with **hydrogen** to form hydrogen iodide. The reaction is **endothermic** and the mixture turns from purple to colourless.

I I + H H → H I H I

a) Which old bonds are broken?

....

b) Which new bonds are made?

....

c) Which of the processes is endothermic — breaking bonds or forming new ones?

....

d) Do you think that the temperature of the reaction vessel will rise or fall during this reaction? Explain your answer.

....

....

Mixed Questions — C2b Topics 4, 5 & 6

Q3 In many reactions, a **catalyst** can be used to increase the **reaction rate**.

a) Explain how a catalyst works.

....

....

b) Which form would be better as a catalyst, a stick or a powder? Explain your answer.

....

....

Q4 Orwell found that **1.4 g** of **silicon** reacted with **7.1 g** of **chlorine** to produce the reactive liquid silicon chloride.

a) Work out the **empirical formula** of the silicon chloride.

....

....

b) Calculate the **percentage mass** of chlorine in silicon chloride.

....

....

c) Write down the balanced chemical equation for the reaction.

....

d) Orwell predicted he would obtain 8.5 g of silicon chloride, however he only obtained 6.5 g. Calculate the percentage yield for this reaction.

....

Q5 **Aqueous chlorine**, Cl_2, was added to **potassium bromide solution**, KBr. Aqueous chlorine is pale green and potassium bromide is colourless.

a) Complete and **balance** the following chemical equation:

Cl_2 + ... KBr $\rightarrow$ .... + ...

b) What would you observe when the two reactants are mixed?

....

c) Suggest why bromine solution will **not** react with aqueous potassium chloride.

....

90

Mixed Questions — C2b Topics 4, 5 & 6

Q6 Metals make up about 80% of all the elements in the periodic table.

a) Shade the area where **transition metals** are found on the periodic table.

b) Read each of the following statements about metals. If the statement is true, tick the box.

☐ Metals are generally malleable.

☐ All metals form coloured compounds.

☐ Metals are insoluble in water.

☐ Generally, metals have low melting and boiling points.

c) Metals are good electrical conductors. Explain why this is the case. You should use ideas about **structure** and **bonding** in your answer.

....

....

....

....

Q7 The elements of **Group 1**, the alkali metals, are **reactive** metals.

a) Choose an **element** from the list to answer each of these questions. Use the periodic table to help you. Give:

i) the element with the lowest density.   ....

ii) the element with the lowest melting point.   ....

iii) the least reactive element.   ....

iv) the element with the largest diameter atoms.   ....

> **A** Rubidium
> **B** Sodium
> **C** Potassium
> **D** Lithium
> **E** Francium
> **F** Caesium

b) Complete the following sentence by circling the correct words.

Group 1 metals react with **water** / **air** to produce **hydrogen** / **oxygen** gas and a **hydroxide** / **chloride** solution. The solutions formed by Group 1 metals in water are **acidic** / **neutral** / **alkaline**.

c) How does the reactivity of the alkali metals change as you move down the group? Explain this trend in terms of electronic configuration.

....

....

....

....

C2b Topic 6 — Quantitative Chemistry

Static Electricity

Q1 Fill in the gaps in these sentences with the words below.

electrons	positive	static	friction	insulating	negative

.... electricity can build up when two ....

materials are rubbed together. The .... moves ....

from one material onto the other. This leaves a .... charge

on one of the materials and a .... charge on the other.

Q2 **Circle** the pairs of charges that would attract each other and **underline** those that would repel.

positive and positive   positive and negative   negative and positive   negative and negative

Q3 The sentences below are wrong. Write out a **correct** version for each.

a) A polythene rod becomes negatively charged when rubbed with a duster because it loses electrons.

....

....

b) The closer two charged objects are together, the less strongly they attract or repel.

....

....

c) A material that loses electrons is left with a positive charge that is twice the lost negative charge.

....

....

Q4 What are the important similarities and differences between:

a) protons and neutrons?

....

....

b) protons and electrons?

....

....

Static Electricity

Q5 Match up these phrases to describe what happens in a **thunderstorm**.
Write out your complete sentences below in the correct order.

If the voltage gets big enough...

... the voltage gets higher and higher.

The bottoms of the clouds become negatively charged...

... and electrons are transferred between them.

As the charge increases...

... there is a huge spark (a flash of lightning).

Raindrops and ice bump together...

... because they gain extra electrons.

1. ....

2. ....

3. ....

4. ....

Q6 Three friends are talking about **static electricity**.

Why does my jumper crackle when I take it off?

Do cotton clothes get charged as much as nylon clothes?

How come I get zapped by my car door every time I get out?

Steph

Dan

Laura

Answer their questions in the spaces below.

Steph: ....

....

Laura: ....

....

Dan: ....

....

Static Electricity

Q7 Tick whether each of these statements is **true** or **false**.

	True	False
a) A charged comb can pick up small pieces of paper if they are placed near it.	☐	☐
b) A charged object can force electrons in an uncharged object to move — this is called induction.	☐	☐
c) Electrically charged objects can attract other objects — but only if they are charged too.	☐	☐

Q8 Jonny walks across a **nylon** carpet wearing **rubber-soled** trainers. When he goes to open the **metal** door handle he gets an electric shock. Explain why.

....

....

....

....

Q9 Wayne rubs a balloon against his nylon sweater.

a) Describe what happens to the **electrons** in the atoms on the surface of his sweater, and the effect this has on the **charge** of the balloon.

....

....

....

....

b) After rubbing the balloon on his sweater, Wayne holds it up against a wall and it sticks. Explain, in terms of charges, why the balloon sticks to the **uncharged** wall.

....

....

....

Top Tips: Static electricity is responsible for many of life's little annoyances — bad hair days, and those little shocks you get from touching car doors and even stroking the cat. Still, it can be kinda cool too — thunderstorms can be spectacular and hours of fun can be had with a balloon...

94

Uses and Dangers of Static Electricity

Q1 Choose from the words below to complete the passage.

fuel   explosion   tankers   wood   petrol   sparks   plastic   earthed

> Static electricity can be dangerous when refuelling aircraft. If too much static builds up, there
> might be .... which could set fire to the ....
> This could lead to an .... To prevent this happening, the nozzle of
> the filler pipe is .... so the charge is conducted away. There are similar
> safety problems with fuel .... and .... stations.

Q2 The sentences below are wrong. Write out a **correct** version for each.

a) Fuel tankers are earthed when refuelling using an insulating strap.

....

....

b) If a positively charged object is connected to earth by a metal strap, electrons flow
through the strap from the object to the ground, and the object is safely discharged.

....

....

Q3 The diagram shows an electrostatic paint sprayer.

a) How do the drops of paint become charged?

....

b) Why does this help produce a fine spray?

....

c) Explain how the paint drops are attracted to the object being sprayed.

....

....

d) Give **one** other use of electrostatic sprayers.

....

P2a Topic 1 — Static and Current Electricity

Charge and Current

Q1 Fill in the gaps in the paragraph with the words below. You may need some words more than once.

time	carried	rate	current	electrons	metals

Electric current is the .... of flow of charge — the amount of

charge that passes a point over a certain amount of ....

Charge has to be .... by something. In ....

the charge carriers are .... — negatively charged particles that are

free to move. Therefore, in these conducting materials, the ....

is simply the flow of ....

Q2 The diagram shows three traces on the same oscilloscope. The settings are the same in each case.

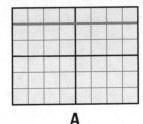 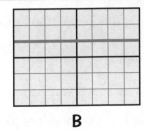 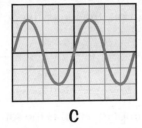

A   B   C

Write down the **letter(s)** of the trace(s) that show:

a) current from an a.c. supply. ....

b) current from a battery. ....

c) the highest d.c. voltage. ....

d) current that flows in only one direction. ....

Q3 The table below shows data from an experiment comparing three lamps, A, B and C.

	Lamp A	Lamp B	Lamp C
Time lamp is switched on (s)	2	4	
Current through lamp (A)	3		2
Charge transferred (C)		12	10

Calculate the **missing values** and write them in the table.

Q4 A 3 volt battery can supply a current of 5 amps for 20 minutes before it needs recharging. Calculate how much charge the battery can provide before it needs recharging.

....

....

....

Electric Current and Potential Difference

Q1   Use the words in the box to fill in the gaps. Use each word once only.

| more   voltage   resistance   less   current   force |

a)   The flow of electrons round a circuit is called the ....

b)   .... is the .... that pushes the current round the circuit.

c)   If you increase the voltage, ... current will flow.

d)   If you increase the ...., ... current will flow.

Remember, voltage and potential difference both mean the same thing.

Q2   The following statements are wrong.
Write out a correct version of each.

a)   In a circuit, the larger the potential difference, the less energy is transferred per unit of charge.

....

....

b)   One ampere (amp) is the same as one coulomb per joule.

....

c)   One volt is the same as one joule per ampere.

....

d)   Voltage is conserved at circuit junctions.

....

Q3   The diagram opposite shows a **parallel** circuit. Ammeter A_2 has a reading of **0.27 A** and A_3 has a reading of **0.43 A**.

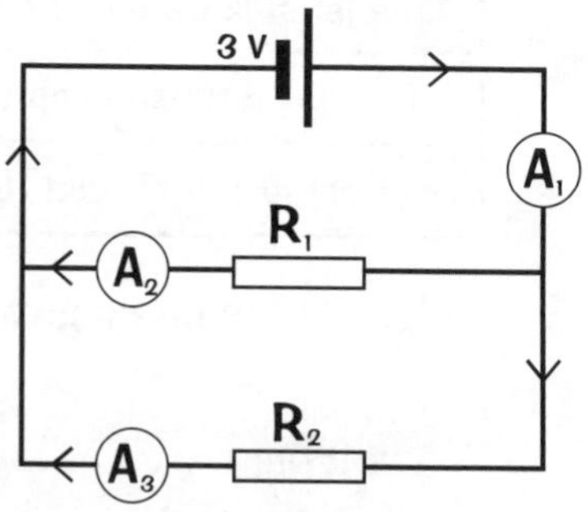

a)   What reading is shown on ammeter A_1?
Circle the correct answer.

        0.16 A   0.7 A   0.43 A

b)   Explain your answer.

....

....

....

Resistance and V = I × R

Q1   Match up these items from a standard test circuit with the **correct description** and **symbol**.

ITEM	DESCRIPTION	SYMBOL
Cell	The item you're testing.	(A)
Variable Resistor	Provides the voltage.	resistor (variable)
Component	Used to alter the current.	cell
Voltmeter	Measures the current.	(V)
Ammeter	Measures the voltage.	resistor

Q2   Write down:

a) the **unit** of:

i) current ....   ii) voltage ....   iii) resistance ....

World's Strongest Current

b) two ways of **decreasing** the current in a standard test circuit:

1. ....

2. ....

Q3   Indicate whether these statements are **true** or **false**.
Write out a **correct version** of the false statements.

		True	False
a)	The current in a circuit can be changed using a variable resistor.	☐	☐
b)	An ammeter should be connected in parallel with a component.	☐	☐
c)	Items that are in series can be in any order.	☐	☐
d)	A voltmeter should be connected in series with a component.	☐	☐

....

....

....

....

Q4   On one particularly rock 'n' roll Saturday night, Jeremy decided to use a standard test circuit to find the resistance of a **fixed resistor**. He found a current of **0.2 A** flowed through the resistor when connected to a **3 V** power supply. Calculate the resistance of the resistor.

....

....

Resistance and V = I × R

Q5 Match the correct label to each of the **V-I graphs** below.

FIXED RESISTOR   FILAMENT LAMP   DIODE

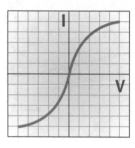   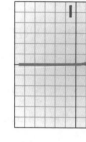   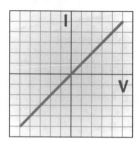

A ....   B ....   C ....

Q6 Indicate whether the following are **true** or **false**.
Write out a **correct version** of the false statements.

		True	False
a)	The resistance of a filament lamp decreases as it gets hot.	☐	☐
b)	A current of 0.5 A will flow through a 2 Ω fixed resistor connected to a 3 V battery.	☐	☐
c)	Current can flow freely through a diode in both directions.	☐	☐
d)	The current through a fixed resistor at constant temperature is proportional to the voltage.	☐	☐
e)	Current can flow both ways through a filament lamp.	☐	☐

....

....

....

....

Q7 The graph below shows V-I curves for four resistors.

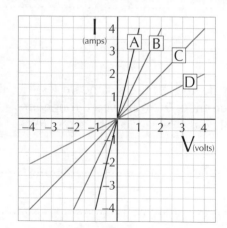

a) Calculate the resistance of resistor C.

....

b) Calculate the resistance of resistor B.

....

c) State which of the four resistors has the highest resistance.

....

You don't have to calculate the resistance of each resistor — think about how the gradient relates to resistance.

P2a Topic 2 — Controlling and Using Electric Current

Devices and Resistance

Q1 Fill in the gaps using the words in the box.

power	current	how long	potential

The total energy transferred by an appliance depends on
.... it's used for and its ....
The power of an appliance can be calculated using the formula:
power = ... difference × ....

Q2 Tick the boxes to show whether the following statements are **true** or **false**.

                                                                  True   False

a) LDRs and thermistors are types of **variable** resistor.

b) An LDR has a **high** resistance in very **bright** light.

c) The resistance of a thermistor **increases** as the temperature **decreases**.

d) An LDR could be part of a useful thermostat.

Q3 Leyla was doing her homework when the **light** on her desk **went out**. Leyla's mum says the **bulb** has blown and needs replacing, but that they should wait till it **cools down** before touching it.

a) Explain what causes the filament in the lamp to get hot when current passes through it. Your answer should include the words **ions**, **electrons** and **lattice**.

....

....

....

b) Why are the filaments in lamps designed to have a very high resistance?

....

....

Top Tips: Wow... power, thermistors, LDRs, current, energy AND resistors — this page really is full to the brim with physics joy. Make sure you know all about power and energy transfer, as well as how electrons heat up a resistor as they travel through it.

P2a Topic 2 — Controlling and Using Electric Current

Devices and Resistance

Q4 An electric heater is rated at **230 V**, **1500 W**.
Calculate the current it uses. Circle the correct answer below.

6.5 A   0.15 A   4.6 A   0.7 A

Q5 Lucy is comparing **three lamps**. She connects each lamp in a circuit and measures the **current**. Her results are shown in the table below.

Complete the table by filling in the missing values.

	Lamp A	Lamp B	Lamp C
Voltage (V)	12	3	230
Current (A)	2.5	4	0.1
Power (W)			
Energy transferred in one minute (J)			

Q6 When a current flows through a resistor, some energy is transferred to the resistor and causes it to **heat up**. Suggest **two** reasons why many electrical devices are designed to **minimise** this heating effect.

1. ....

....

2. ....

....

Q7 Dale loves a bit of DIY, and is drilling holes to put up some shelves.
His electric drill is attached to a **12 V** battery and uses a current of **2.3 A**.

a) Write down the equation that relates current, voltage, electrical energy transferred and time.

....

b) If it takes Dale 30 seconds to drill one hole, how much energy will be transferred by the motor if he drills **eight** holes?

....

....

Velocity and Acceleration

Q1 Which of the following are **vector quantities**? Circle the correct answers.

displacement   speed   velocity

distance   acceleration

Q2 A pulse of laser light takes 1.3 seconds to travel from the Moon to the Earth. The speed of light is approximately 3×10^8 m/s. How far away is the Moon from the Earth? Give your answer in km.

....

....

....

Q3 Ealing is about 12 km west of Marble Arch. It takes a tube train 20 minutes to get to Marble Arch from Ealing.

Only **one** of the following statements is true. Circle the appropriate letter.

    A   The average speed of the train is 60 m/s.

    B   The average velocity of the train is 10 m/s.

    C   The average velocity of the train is 60 m/s due east.

    D   The average speed of the train is 10 m/s.

    E   The average velocity of the train is 10 m/s due west.

Q4 An egg is dropped from the top of the Eiffel tower. It hits the ground after **8 seconds**, at a speed of **80 m/s**.

a) Calculate the egg's acceleration.

....

b) How long did it take for the egg to reach a velocity of 40 m/s?

....

Q5 A car accelerates at **2 m/s²**. After **4 seconds** it reaches a speed of **24 m/s**.

How fast was it going before it started to accelerate?

....

....

D-T and V-T Graphs

Q1 Steve walked to football training only to find that he'd left his boots at home.
He turned round and walked back home, where he spent 30 seconds looking for
them. To make it to training on time he had to run back at twice his walking speed.

Below is an incomplete **distance-time graph** for Steve's journey.

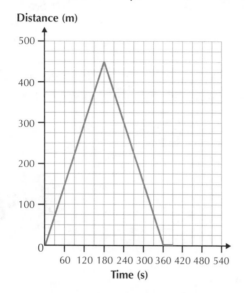

a) How long did it take Steve to walk to training?

....

b) Calculate Steve's speed (in m/s) as he
walked to training.

....

....

c) Complete the graph to show Steve's run back
from his house to training (with his boots).

Q2 The distance-time graph and the velocity-time graph below both indicate the **same** three journeys.

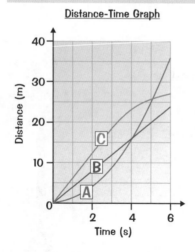

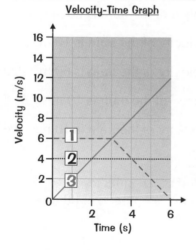

Draw lines to show how the
distance-time and velocity-time
graphs match up.

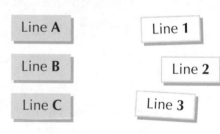

Line **A**   Line **1**

Line **B**   Line **2**

Line **C**   Line **3**

Q3 The velocity-time graph on the right shows the
journeys of three different cyclists, A, B and C.

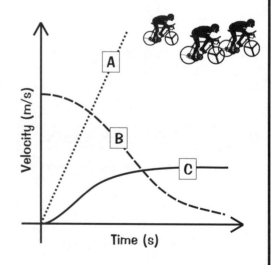

a) Which cyclist is decelerating?   ....

b) Which cyclist reaches a constant velocity?   ....

c) Which cyclist has the largest acceleration? ....

d) Which cyclist has the lowest final velocity? ....

e) Which cyclist has a constant acceleration?   ....

D-T and V-T Graphs

Q4 Below is a velocity-time graph for the descent of a lunar lander.
It accelerates due to the pull of gravity from the Moon.

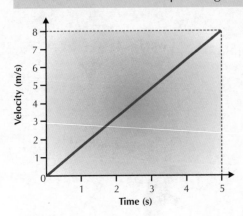

a) Use the graph to calculate
the lander's acceleration.

....

b) Calculate the distance travelled by the lander during
the five seconds of descent shown on the graph.

....

....

Q5 The speed limit for cars on motorways is
70 mph (about 31 m/s). A motorist was
stopped by the police for speeding as she
joined the motorway from a service station.

The distance-time graph on the right shows
the car's motion. The motorist denied
speeding. Was she telling the truth?

....

....

Distance (m)

(graph with axes: Distance (m) from 0 to 72, Time (s) from 0 to 3.0)

Time (s)

Q6 A motorist saw a kitten on the road 25 m in front of him. It took him 0.75 seconds to react
and slam on the brakes. The velocity-time graph below shows the car's deceleration.

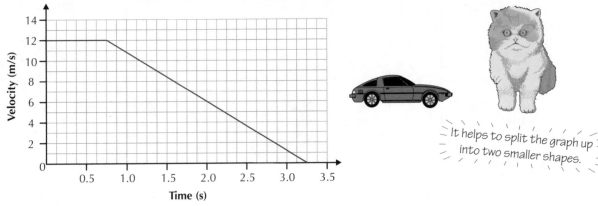

*It helps to split the graph up
into two smaller shapes.*

The kitten doesn't move from its spot.
Use the graph to work out whether the motorist stopped before hitting the kitten.

....

....

Top Tips: Don't let distance-time or velocity-time graphs get the better of you
— break them down into separate chunks and they'll be a whole lot easier to work out.

Forces

Q1 The forces acting on a balloon floating at a constant height are shown by the **force diagram** below.

The sentences below describe the balloon's motion.
Circle the correct word(s) in each sentence.

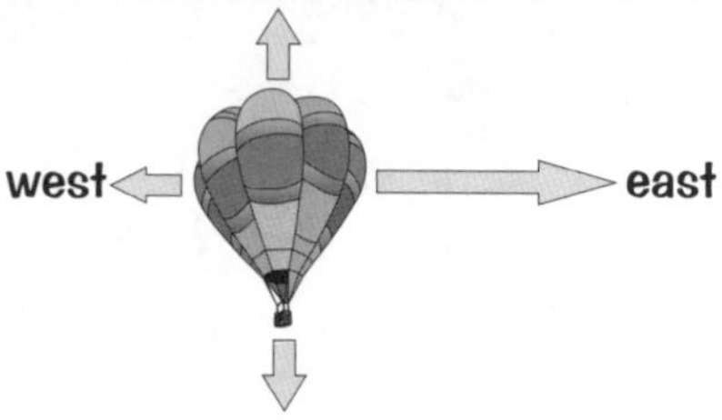

a) There is a greater driving force in the **east /** ~~west~~ direction.

b) The balloon will **rise /** ~~fall~~ **/ stay at the same height**.

Q2 A bear rides a bike north at a constant speed.

a) Label the forces acting on the bear.

upthrust

air resistance forward

driving force

weight

b) The bear brakes and slows down.
Are the forces balanced **as** he slows
down? If not, which direction is the
overall force in?

from back to front

Q3 A teapot sits on a table.

a) Explain why it **doesn't** sink into the table.

....

b) Jane picks up the teapot and hangs it from the ceiling.
Label the forces acting on the teapot suspended by the rope on the picture below.

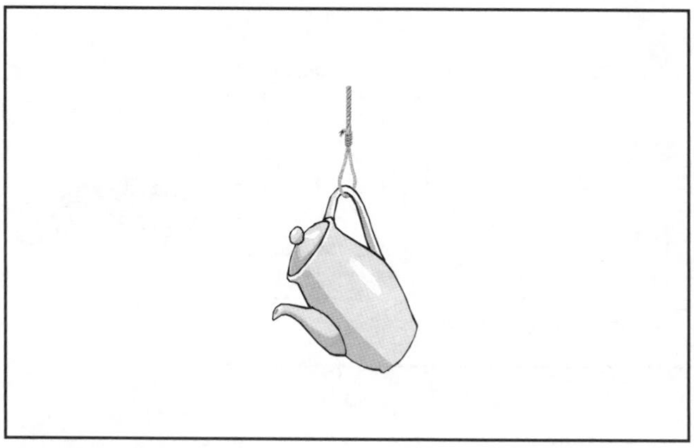

Show the direction of each force and make sure the size of each arrow relates to the size of the force.

c) The rope breaks and the teapot accelerates towards the floor.

i) Are the vertical forces balanced? Explain your answer.

....

ii) The teapot hits the floor without breaking and bounces upwards.
Which force causes the teapot to bounce upwards?

....

Weight and Terminal Velocity

Q1 Use the words supplied to fill in the blanks in the paragraph.

terminal	balances	increases	constant	greater	accelerates

An object is dropped from a height and falls through the atmosphere. At first, its weight is

.... than the air resistance acting on it, so it ....

downwards. As its speed increases, the air resistance .... until it

.... its weight. At this point, its velocity is .... — its

acceleration is zero and the object is said to have reached its .... velocity.

Q2 Two mad scientists are planning a trip to Mars.

a) Professor White tells Professor Brown —

"We won't need so much fuel for the return trip — the rocket will have less mass on Mars."

Is Professor White's reasoning correct? Explain your answer.

....

....

b) Professor Brown wants to investigate gravity on Mars. He takes to Mars a small fire extinguisher which weighs 50 N on Earth. He also takes his Newton scales.

On Mars, Professor Brown weighs the fire extinguisher.
The scales read **19 N**.
Calculate the **gravitational field strength** on Mars.

Find the mass of the fire extinguisher first. Remember that on Earth, g = 10 N/kg.

....

....

Q3 A scientist plans to travel to the moon to perform an experiment. He will drop a **hammer** and a **feather** from the same height.

The moon's atmosphere is so thin you can treat it as a vacuum.

The scientist hypothesises that if he dropped both at the same time, the hammer would land before the feather. Is he correct? Explain your answer.

....

....

....

....

Forces and Motion

Q1 a) Tick the correct boxes to show whether the sentences are true or false.

True False

   i) A resultant force is the overall force acting on a body. ☐ ☐

   ii) An object will remain stationary if there is zero resultant force acting on it. ☐ ☐

   iii) For an object to keep travelling at a steady speed, it must have an overall force acting on it. ☐ ☐

   iv) If all the forces on an object are balanced, it is said to have a resultant force acting on it. ☐ ☐

b) Write a correct version of each false sentence in the space below. ☐ ☐

....

....

....

....

Q2 A **flamingo** is standing on one leg.

a) Two forces, A and B, are shown on the diagram to the right. Label the force marked B.

b) Complete the following sentences about the two forces:

> Force A is exerted by the .... on the
>
> .... Force B is exerted by the
>
> .... on the ....

c) Are force A and force B equal in size? Explain your answer.

....

....

Q3 Otto is driving the school bus at a **steady speed** along a level road.
Tick the boxes next to any of the following statements which are **true**.

☐ The driving force of the engine is bigger than the friction and air resistance combined.

☐ The driving force of the engine is equal to the friction and air resistance combined.

☐ There are no forces acting on the bus.

☐ No force is required to keep the bus moving.

Forces and Motion

Q4 Complete the following passage.

When an object exerts a .... on another object, it experiences a force in return. For example, if Martin leans on a wall with a force of 150 N, the wall exerts a force of .... N in the opposite direction — an '................................ and ....' reaction. The force Martin exerts is called the .... force and the force the wall exerts is called the .... force.

Q5 Which of the following statements correctly explains what happens when you walk? Circle the appropriate letter.

A   Your feet push the ground backwards, so the ground pushes you forwards.

B   The force in your muscles overcomes the friction between your feet and the ground.

C   The ground's reaction can't push you backwards because of friction.

D   Your feet push forwards, and the ground's reaction is upwards.

Q6 Kate and William are having a bit of a skate. William gives Kate a push with a force 250 N.

a) Give the force of Kate on William.

....

b) Who will accelerate the most? Explain your answer.

....

....

....

....

....

Top Tips: Remember that force is a vector quantity — it has a magnitude (an amount) and a direction. This is particularly important when drawing and interpreting force diagrams. Whenever one force acts, you get another one acting in the opposite direction. You can see this for yourself the next time you go swimming — when you push the water backwards, the water pushes you forwards.

P2a Topic 3 — Motion and Forces

Force and Acceleration

Q1   Use the words below to fill in the blanks. You won't have to use all the words.

mass	force	accelerates	opposite	resultant	inversely

If an object has a .... force acting on it, it ....

in the direction of the .... The acceleration depends on the size

of the force and on the .... of the object.

Q2   State whether the **forces** acting on these objects are **balanced**
(zero resultant force) or **unbalanced**. Explain your answers.

a)   A **cricket ball** slowing down as it rolls along the outfield.

....

b)   A **vase** knocked off a window ledge.

....

c)   A **bag of rubbish** which was ejected from a spacecraft in empty space.

....

Q3   The table below shows the **masses** and **maximum accelerations** of four different antique cars.

Write down the names of the four cars
in order of increasing driving force.

1. ....

2. ....

3. ....

4. ....

Car	Mass (kg)	Maximum acceleration (m/s^2)
Disraeli 9000	800	5
Palmerston 6i	1560	0.7
Heath TT	950	3
Asquith 380	790	2

Q4   Jo and Bob's scooters have the same engine. Bob and his scooter have a combined mass of 110 kg
and an acceleration of 2.80 m/s^2. On her scooter, Jo only manages an acceleration of 1.71 m/s^2.

a)   What **force** can the engine exert?

....

b)   Calculate the combined mass of Jo and her scooter.

....

Force and Acceleration

Q5 Maisie drags a **1 kg** mass along a table with a newton meter so that it accelerates at **0.25 m/s²**. The newton meter reads **0.4 N**. Calculate the force of friction between the mass and the table.

....

....

Q6 A camper van of mass 2500 kg drives along a straight, level road at a constant speed.

a) At this speed, air resistance is 2000 N and the friction between the wheel bearings is 500 N.

i) What force is the engine exerting? ....

....

ii) Draw a diagram to show
all the horizontal forces
acting on the camper van.
Give the size of each force.

b) A strong headwind begins blowing, with a force of **200 N**.
The van slows down. Calculate its deceleration.

....

Q7 Jen and Sarah conduct an experiment to investigate the relationship between **force** and **acceleration**. They set up the experimental apparatus shown below.

a) Explain what the masses attached to the trolley are used for.

....

....

b) Describe how the **light gate** and **data logging software** are used in the investigation.

....

....

....

c) Describe the **relationship** between force and acceleration you would expect them to find.

....

....

Mixed Questions — P2a Topics 1, 2 & 3

Q1 Norman loves trainspotting. As a special treat, he not only notes the train numbers but plots a **distance-time** graph for two of the trains.

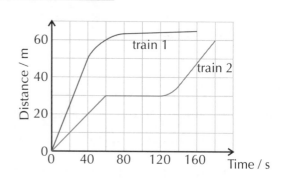

a) For how long is train 2 stationary?

....

b) Both trains start at a steady speed. How can you tell this from the graph?

....

c) Calculate the initial speed of the faster train.

....

d) Describe the motion of train 1 between 40 s and 80 s.

....

Q2 In the film 'Crouching Sparrow, Hidden Beaver', a dummy is dropped from the top of a building.

a) Sketch a distance-time graph and a velocity-time graph for the dummy from the moment it is dropped until just after it hits the ground. (Ignore air resistance and assume the dummy does not reach a terminal velocity.)

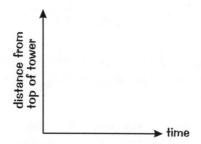
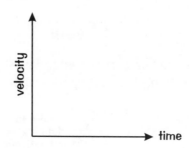

b) Do any forces act on the dummy when it lies still on the ground (after falling)? If so, what are they?

....

c) The take doesn't go to plan so the dummy is lifted back to the top of the building using a 760 W motor. If the motor uses the mains voltage (**230 V**), calculate the current through it.

....

d) The film's director decides to use a taller building for the scene. Falling from this new building, the dummy reaches its terminal velocity. Explain what is meant by 'terminal velocity'.

....

....

....

Mixed Questions — P2a Topics 1, 2 & 3

Q3 Scott water-skis over a 100 m course. When he reaches the end of the course, Scott lets go of the tow rope.

a) The graph below shows how Scott's velocity changed over the course.
Describe his **acceleration**:

  i) between 0 and 5 seconds,

  ....

  ii) between 5 and 22 seconds,

  ....

  iii) after 30 seconds.

  ....

b) How far did Scott travel in the first 20 seconds?

....

....

c) A newton meter on the tow rope registers that Scott is being pulled with a force of 475 N.
What was the **total combined force** of air resistance and friction between his
water skis and the water between 10 and 25 seconds? Explain your answer.

....

....

Q4 Paul sets off from a junction on his scooter which produces a thrust of 270 N. The total mass of Paul and his scooter is 180 kg. For the following questions, assume air resistance is negligible.

a) Calculate the initial acceleration of Paul's scooter.

....

b) Calculate the size of the force produced when Paul applies his brakes and decelerates at **5 m/s²**.

....

c) Paul had reached a speed of **17.5 m/s** before he began to decelerate.
Assuming he decelerates steadily, how many seconds will it take him to stop completely?

....

d) Paul picks up a large package and carries it on his scooter. Calculate the mass of the package if his initial acceleration when he sets off again is **1.45 m/s²**, but the thrust of the scooter remains **270 N**.

....

....

Mixed Questions — P2a Topics 1, 2 & 3

Q5 The diagram shows an aircraft being refuelled.
No safety precautions have been taken.

a) **i)** Explain how static electricity could cause an explosion in this situation.

....

....

ii) Give one precaution that can be taken to avoid this danger.

....

b) Write down one example of how static electricity is **useful**.

....

Q6 A temperature sensor containing a thermistor is used to monitor the temperature of a room. The sensor is connected to a circuit containing a filament bulb.
As the temperature increases, the bulb's brightness increases.

a) What is a thermistor?

....

b) Explain why the filament in the bulb glows when a current flows through it.

....

....

....

c) The filament bulb is connected to a 25 V electricity supply.

i) Calculate the resistance of the filament bulb if it has a current of 4 A flowing through it.

....

ii) Calculate how much energy is transferred by the bulb over a time period of **5 minutes**.

....

....

iii) Calculate how much charge passes through the bulb in this time.

....

d) The sensor uses a **d.c.** electricity supply. Explain, in terms of charge carriers, what this means.

....

....

Stopping Distances

Q1 **Stopping distance** and **braking distance** are **not** the same thing.

a) What is meant by 'braking distance'?

....

b) Use the words below to complete the following sentences.

braking   noticing   react   thinking   hazard

i) Thinking distance is the distance travelled in the time it takes a driver to ....

ii) Reaction time is the time between a driver .... a ....
and applying the brakes.

iii) Stopping distance = ... distance + ... distance.

Q2 Will the following factors affect **thinking** distance, **braking** distance or **both**?
Write them in the relevant columns of the table.

tiredness   road surface   weather   speed   diesel spills
alcohol   tyre tread   brakes   mass of the vehicle   ice

Thinking Distance	Braking Distance

Q3 Beth wants to make a toy car race track. To help her decide which material to use, she finds the **force** needed to slide a 1 kg rubber block across a flat surface covered in three different materials. The table below shows her results.

a) What force opposes the block sliding? ....

b) Beth wants the toy cars to be able to grip well to the track.
Which of the surfaces tested should she use to make the race track?
Explain your answer.

Material .... because ....

....

....

Material	Force needed for block to slide
1	60 N
2	5 N
3	24 N

Q4 A car has just been driven through a **deep puddle**, making the brakes wet. Explain why this will **increase** the **stopping distance** of the car.

....

....

114

Car Safety

Q1 Circle the correct words or phrases to make the following statements true.

a) If the velocity of a moving object doubles, its **kinetic energy** / **momentum** will double.

b) If you drop a suitcase out of a moving car, the car's momentum will **decrease** / **increase**.

c) When two objects collide the total momentum **changes** / **stays the same**.

d) When a force acts on an object its momentum **changes** / **stays the same**.

Q2 Place the following four trucks in order of increasing momentum.

Truck A	**Truck B**	**Truck C**	**Truck D**
speed = 30 m/s	speed = 10 m/s	speed = 20 m/s	speed = 15 m/s
mass = 3000 kg	mass = 4500 kg	mass = 4000 kg	mass = 3500 kg

....

....

....

(lowest momentum) .... , ... , ... , ... (highest momentum)

Q3 Shopping trolley A has a mass of 10 kg and is moving east at 4 m/s. It collides with trolley B which has a mass of 30 kg and is moving west at 1 m/s. The two trolleys join together.

a) Complete the diagram showing the masses and velocities of the trolleys **before** they collide.

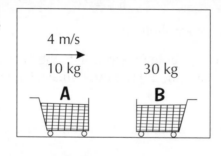

For this one you'll need to know the _total momentum_ of the two trolleys _before_ the collision.

b) Find the **velocity** of the trolleys **after** the collision (when they are joined) and draw a diagram showing their speed and direction.

....

....

....

....

P2b Topic 4 — Momentum, Energy, Work and Power

Car Safety

Q4 A 750 kg car is travelling at 30 m/s along the motorway. It crashes into the barrier of the central reservation and is stopped in a period of 1.2 seconds.

a) Find the size of the **average force** acting on the car to stop it.

....

....

b) Explain why the occupants of the car are likely to be less severely injured if they are wearing seat belts made of slightly **stretchy** material.

....

....

Q5 A 0.15 kg cricket ball is dropped vertically onto a floor. It hits the floor at a speed of 10 m/s and bounces vertically back up at the same speed. If the ball is in contact with the floor for 0.02 s, what is the average force exerted on it?

How does the ball's velocity change?

....

....

....

....

Q6 Simon is investigating **crumple zones** using the apparatus shown on the right.

Simon fits the front of a trolley with different materials to make different 'crumple zones'. For each test, the trolley starts **at rest** at the **same position** on the slope and rolls towards the force sensor. The **mass** of the trolley is the **same** in each test. Simon records the **maximum force** of the trolley on the sensor, and **how long** each collision lasts for in the table below.

Crumple zone	Maximum force during the collision (N)	Collision time (s)
1	10	0.8
2	40	0.2
3	16	0.5

Which of Simon's crumple zones was the most effective? Explain your answer.

....

....

....

Work and Power

Q1 Circle the correct words to make the following sentences true.

a) Work involves the transfer of **force** / **heat** / **energy**.

b) To do work **a force** / **an acceleration** must act over a **distance** / **time**.

c) Work is measured in **watts** / **joules**.

Q2 Indicate whether the following statements are **true** or **false**.

	True	False
a) Work is done when a toy car is pushed along the ground.	☐	☐
b) No work is done if a force is applied to an object which does not move.	☐	☐
c) Gravity does work on an apple that is not moving.	☐	☐
d) Gravity does work on an apple that falls out of a tree.	☐	☐

Q3 Complete this passage by using the words provided.

heat	energy	100	rate	light	watts	joules

Power is the .... of doing work, or how much .... is

transferred per second. It is measured in .... or .... per

second. A 100 W light bulb transfers .... joules of electrical energy into

.... and .... each second.

Q4 An elephant exerts a constant force of **1200 N** to push a donkey along a track at a steady **1 m/s**.

a) Write down the equation that links force, distance and work done.

....

b) Calculate the work done by the elephant if the donkey moves **8 m**.

....

c) From where does the elephant get the energy to do this work? ....

d) Into what form(s) is this energy transferred when work is done on the donkey?

....

Top Tips: Power is a measure of the energy transferred, or work done, within a certain time — the faster a person or machine can get a task done, the more powerful it is. Just think, if you were a power-mad ruler you could try take over the world in the blink of an eye, mwah haa ha ha ha...

P2b Topic 4 — Momentum, Energy, Work and Power

Work and Power

Q5 Ben's mass is 60 kg. He climbs a ladder. The rungs of the ladder are 20 cm apart.

a) What force(s) is Ben doing work **against** as he climbs?

....

b) As he climbs, what happens to the **energy** supplied by Ben's muscles?

....

....

20 cm

c) How much work does Ben do when he climbs **10 rungs**? (Ignore any 'wasted' energy.)
Assume that g = 10 N/kg.

....

....

d) How many rungs of the ladder must Ben climb before he has done **15 kJ** of work?
(Ignore any 'wasted' energy.) Assume that g = 10 N/kg.

....

....

Q6 Catherine and Sally decide to run up a set of stairs to see who can get to the top more quickly. At the top of the stairs, Catherine has a gravitational potential energy of **2300 J**, and Sally has a gravitational potential energy of **2400 J**.

Catherine won the race in **6.2 s**, while Sally took **6.4 s**.
Which girl generated more **power**?

....

....

Q7 Tom likes to build model boats. His favourite boat is the Carter, which has a motor power of **150 W**.

a) How much **energy** does the Carter transfer in **10 minutes**?

....

b) The petrol for the boat's motor can supply **30 kJ/ml**.
What volume of petrol is used up in **10 minutes**?

....

c) Tom decides to get a model speed boat which transfers **120 kJ** in 10 minutes.
What is the **power** of the engine?

....

Kinetic and Potential Energy

Q1 Indicate whether the following statements are **true** or **false**.

		True	False
a)	Gravitational potential energy = mass × g × height.	☺	☹
b)	Kinetic energy is energy due to an object's position.	☺	☹
c)	On Earth, the gravitational field strength is approximately **20 N/kg**.	☺	☹
d)	The kinetic energy of an object depends on its velocity.	☺	☹
e)	Brakes convert kinetic energy into mostly heat energy to slow down a car.	☺	☹

Q2 Dave works at a DIY shop. He has to load **28** flagstones onto the delivery truck. Each flagstone has a mass of **25 kg** and has to be lifted **1.2 m** onto the truck.

a) How much gravitational potential energy does one flagstone gain when lifted onto the truck? (g = 10 N/kg)

....

b) What is the **total gravitational potential energy** gained by the flagstones after they are all loaded onto the truck?

....

Q3 A large truck and a car both have a kinetic energy of **614 400 J**. The mass of the truck is **12 288 kg** and the car **1200 kg**.

a) Calculate the **speed** of:

i) the car ....

ii) the truck ....

b) John is playing with his remote-controlled toy car and truck. The car's mass is 100 g. The truck's mass is 300 g. The car is moving twice as fast as the truck. Which has more kinetic energy — the car or the truck? Explain your answer.

....

....

Q4 Jack rides his bicycle along a level road and has a total kinetic energy of **1440 J**. He brakes, exerting a force of **200 N** on the wheels. How far does he travel before he stops?

....

Top Tips: My physics teacher once said I had lots of potential... thanks to being sat on an exceptionally tall stool. Ah, physics jokes... you've got to love 'em. Kinetic energy and gravitational potential energy crop up everywhere, so make sure you get friendly with their formulas.

Conservation of Energy

Q1 A toy cricket ball hit straight upwards has a gravitational potential energy of **242 J** at the **top** of its flight.

a) What is the ball's **kinetic energy just** before it hits the ground? ....

b) Calculate the speed of the ball at this time if its mass is **100 g**.

....

Q2 Mr Coles is about to demonstrate the **conservation of energy**. He holds a heavy pendulum up by a window and lets go.

a) Explain why he can be sure that the pendulum won't smash the window when it swings back.

....

....

b) When the pendulum actually does swing back, it doesn't quite reach the height of the window again. Where has the gravitational potential energy gone?

....

Q3 Dave the frog **jumps** off the ground at a speed of 10 m/s.

a) If Dave has a mass of 500 g, what is his kinetic energy as he leaves the ground?

....

b) What is Dave's maximum possible gravitational potential energy?

....

c) What is the maximum height Dave can reach?

....

d) In practice, why won't Dave reach this height? (Explain your answer in terms of energy.)

....

....

Q4 Kim dives off a **5 m** high diving board and belly-flops into the swimming pool below.

a) If Kim's mass is 100 kg, calculate her kinetic energy as she hits the water.

....

b) At what speed will Kim be falling as she hits the water?

....

Radioactivity

Q1   Fill in the blanks using the words below. Each word should be used only once.

alpha	element	protons	neutrons	nuclei	gamma	radioactive

Isotopes are atoms which have the same number of .... but different numbers

of ....   Some isotopes are .... Their ....

are unstable, so they break down and emit either ...., beta or

.... radiation. When isotopes break down in this way, the nucleus often

changes into that of a new ....

Q2   Indicate whether these sentences are **true** or **false**.

True   False

a)   The number of protons in an atom is known as its atomic number.   ☐   ☐

b)   The number of neutrons in an atom is known as its mass number.   ☐   ☐

c)   Atoms of the same element with the same
     number of neutrons are called isotopes.   ☐   ☐

d)   Radioactive decay speeds up at higher temperatures.   ☐   ☐

Q3   For each of the following isotopes, state the **number of protons** and the **number of neutrons**.

a) $^{3}_{1}\text{H}$

b) $^{14}_{6}\text{C}$

c) $^{14}_{7}\text{N}$

d) $^{16}_{8}\text{O}$

Protons: ....

Neutrons: ....

Protons: ....

Neutrons: ....

Protons: ....

Neutrons: ....

Protons: ....

Neutrons: ....

Q4   An atom is bombarded with ionising radiation.
Explain how the following could **ionise** the atom:

a)   An **alpha** particle passing close by.

....

....

b)   A **beta** particle passing close by.

....

....

Radioactivity

Q5 Complete the table below to show the properties of alpha, beta and gamma radiation.

Radiation Type	What is it?	Ionising power weak/moderate/strong	Penetrating power low/moderate/high
alpha			
beta			
gamma			

Q6 a) For each sentence, tick the correct box to show whether it is **true** or **false**.

True False

i) All nuclear radiation is positively charged. ☐ ☐

ii) Gamma radiation can pass through thin sheets of metal. ☐ ☐

iii) Alpha is the slowest and most strongly ionising type of radiation. ☐ ☐

iv) Beta particles are electrons, so they do not come from the nucleus. ☐ ☐

b) For each of the false sentences, write out a correct version.

....

....

....

Q7 Radiation from three sources — A, B and C, was directed towards target sheets of **paper**, **aluminium** and **lead**. Counters were used to detect where radiation passed through the target sheets.

Source A — the radiation was partially absorbed by the lead.
Source B — the radiation was stopped by the paper.
Source C — the radiation was stopped by the aluminium.

paper   3 mm aluminium   1 cm lead

A

B

C

Radioactive sources

What type of radiation is emitted by:

source A? ...., source B? ...., source C? ....

Nuclear Fission

Q1 Many nuclear power stations split **uranium-235** nuclei in their reactors.

a) **Daughter nuclei** such as barium and krypton are **products** of the fission of uranium-235. Give **two other** products of the fission reaction.

1. .... 2. ....

b) Describe how a fission chain reaction is created in a nuclear reactor.

....

....

....

....

Q2 The diagram below shows how energy from a nuclear reactor generates electricity.

a) Describe how heat energy from the reactor is used to generate electricity.

....

....

b) What causes the reactor to get hot?

....

c) What can be used in a nuclear reactor to slow down neutrons for nuclear fission?

....

d) i) Explain how the control rods control the rate of fission.

....

....

ii) What material are control rods usually made from? ....

e) What could happen if the chain reaction in a nuclear reactor wasn't checked and controlled?

....

....

Nuclear Fusion

Q1 Decide whether the following statements are **true** or **false**.
Write out the correct version of any false statements.

	True	False

a) Nuclear fusion involves small nuclei joining together. ☐ ☐

b) A nuclear fission reaction releases more energy than a nuclear fusion reaction. ☐ ☐

c) Fusion reactors produce very little radioactive waste. ☐ ☐

d) Only a few experimental fusion reactors are generating electricity. ☐ ☐

....

....

Q2 The energy released in stars comes from fusion.

a) **i)** Write down two conditions needed for fusion to take place.

1. .... 2. ....

ii) Explain why these extreme conditions are necessary.

....

b) Fusion reactors are extremely hard to build.

i) Why can the hydrogen used not be held in a physical container?

....

ii) How do fusion reactors get around this problem?

....

c) Describe the main problem with the amount of energy a fusion reactor needs to operate.

....

Q3 In 1989 two scientists claimed to have created energy through **cold fusion**.

a) In what ways did they say cold fusion was different from previous ideas about nuclear fusion?

....

b) Explain why the theory has not been accepted by the scientific community.

....

....

....

....

Background Radiation and Half-life

Q1   Use the words in the box to fill in the gaps in the paragraph below.

| becquerels | half-life | decreases | zero |
| second | undecayed | Geiger-Muller | |

The activity of a radioactive source .... over time as the radioactive

nuclei decay. However, the activity never reaches .... , so scientists

use the idea of .... to measure how quickly the activity falls. This is

the time it takes for half the .... nuclei in a radioactive substance to

decay. Activity is measured in .... — 1 Bq is one decay per

.... , which can be measured using a .... tube.

Q2   Which of the following are **true**? Circle the appropriate letters.

A   About half of the UK's background radiation comes from radon gas.

B   Human activity doesn't contribute to background radiation.

C   If there were no radioactive substances on Earth, there would be no background radiation.

D   Cosmic rays from the Sun are a form of low-level background radiation.

Q3   The concentration of **radon** gas found in people's homes varies across the UK. Why does the concentration vary across the country?

....

....

Q4   A radioactive isotope has a half-life of **60 years**.
Which of these statements describes this isotope correctly? Tick one box only.

In 60 years, half of the atoms in the material will have gone.   ☐

In 30 years' time, only half the atoms will be radioactive.   ☐

In 60 years' time, the activity will be half what it is now.   ☐

In about 180 years there will be almost no radioactivity left in the material.   ☐

Q5   The half-life of uranium-238 is **4500 million** years. The half-life of carbon-14 is **5730** years. If you start with a sample of each element and the two samples have equal initial activity, which will lose its radioactivity most quickly? Circle the correct answer.

uranium-238   carbon-14

Calculating Half-life

Q1 The graph shows how the activity of a radioactive isotope declines with time.

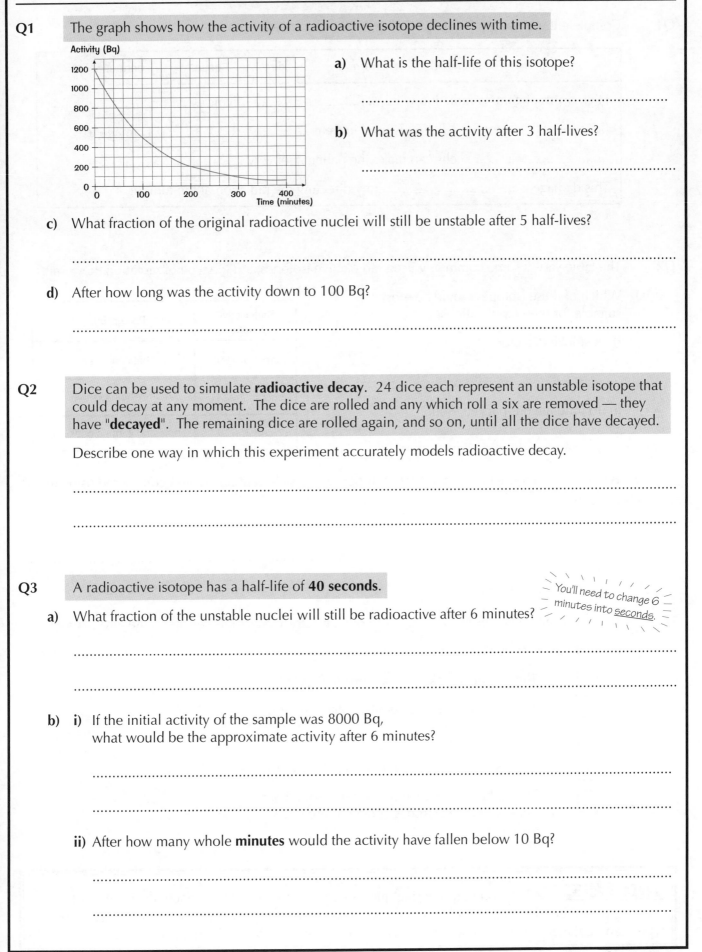

a) What is the half-life of this isotope?

....

b) What was the activity after 3 half-lives?

....

c) What fraction of the original radioactive nuclei will still be unstable after 5 half-lives?

....

d) After how long was the activity down to 100 Bq?

....

....

Q2 Dice can be used to simulate **radioactive decay**. 24 dice each represent an unstable isotope that could decay at any moment. The dice are rolled and any which roll a six are removed — they have "**decayed**". The remaining dice are rolled again, and so on, until all the dice have decayed.

Describe one way in which this experiment accurately models radioactive decay.

....

....

Q3 A radioactive isotope has a half-life of **40 seconds**.

You'll need to change 6 minutes into seconds.

a) What fraction of the unstable nuclei will still be radioactive after 6 minutes?

....

....

b) i) If the initial activity of the sample was 8000 Bq, what would be the approximate activity after 6 minutes?

....

....

ii) After how many whole **minutes** would the activity have fallen below 10 Bq?

....

....

Uses of Radioactivity

Q1 Complete the following paragraph using the words provided.

ill	minimised	normal	kill	cells	cancer

High doses of gamma radiation will .... living ....

Because of this, gamma radiation is used to treat .... Damage to

.... cells can make the patient feel very ....

This damage is .... by directing the radiation at the tumour.

Q2 The table shows some commonly used radioactive isotopes and the type of radiation they emit.

a) Which of these isotopes would be most suitable for these applications?

  i) A smoke detector.

  ....

  ii) To irradiate pre-packed food.

  ....

Radioactive isotope	Decays by...
strontium-90	beta emission
americium-241	mainly alpha emission
cobalt-60	beta and gamma emission

b) What further information about these isotopes would you want before you considered using them?

....

....

Q3 The following sentences explain how a smoke detector works, but they are in the wrong order.

Put them in order by labelling them 1 (first) to 5 (last).

[ ] The circuit is broken so no current flows.

[1] The radioactive source emits alpha particles.

[ ] The alarm sounds.

[ ] A fire starts and smoke particles absorb the alpha radiation.

[ ] The alpha particles cause ionisation of the air between two electrodes and a current flows.

Top Tips: When you're answering questions about the uses of radioactivity, it's important that you remember the properties of the different types of ionising radiation. Each of the three types can be dangerous if used incorrectly, but pretty darned useful in the right scenario.

P2b Topic 6 — Using Radioactive Materials

Uses of Radioactivity

Q4 The diagram shows how **beta radiation** can be used in the control of paper thickness in a paper mill.

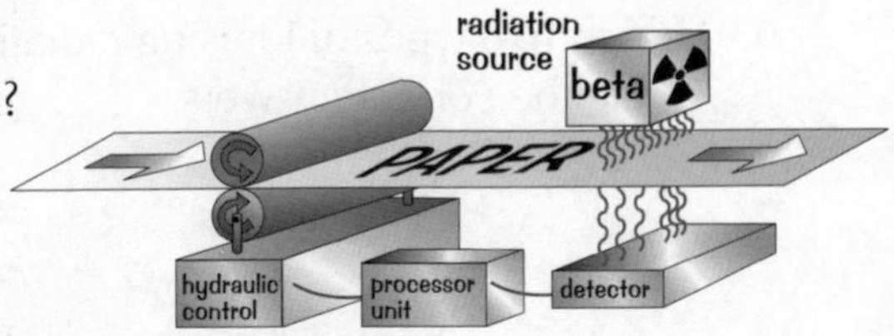

Why is beta radiation used rather than alpha or gamma?

....

....

....

Q5 Radiation can be used to **sterilise** surgical instruments.

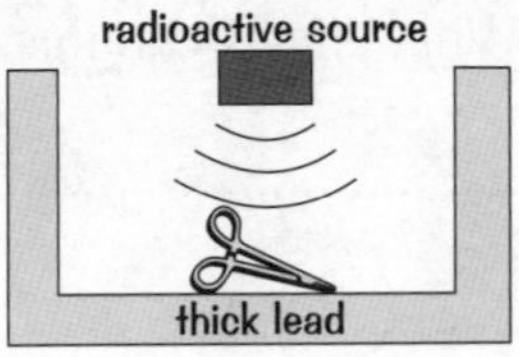

a) What kind of radioactive source is used, and why?
In your answer, mention the **type** of radiation emitted (alpha, beta and gamma) and the **half-life** of the source.

....

....

....

b) What is the purpose of the **thick lead**?

....

c) Similar machines can be used to treat **fruit** before it is exported from South America to Europe, to stop it going bad on the long journey. How does irradiating the fruit help?

....

....

Q6 There will often be an **increased** blood flow to the part of the body where there is a cancerous tumour.

a) Describe how a radioactive tracer can be used to diagnose medical problems such as cancer.

....

....

....

b) What should the **half-life** of the radioactive isotope used in the tracer be, and what **type** of radiation should it emit? Explain your answers.

....

....

....

Dangers of Radioactivity

Q1 The three different types of ionising radiation can all be dangerous.

a) Which **two** types of ionising radiation can pass through the human body?
Circle the correct answers.

alpha   beta   gamma

b) **i)** Which type of radiation is usually most dangerous if it's inhaled or swallowed?

....

ii) What effects can this type of radiation have on the human body?

....

....

....

Q2 Give **four precautions** you should take when working with **radioactive sources** in the laboratory.

1. ....

2. ....

3. ....

4. ....

Q3 When the radioactive substance **radium** was first discovered, it was used to make luminous paint, which was used in the manufacture of glow-in-the-dark watches.

a) Explain why this was **extremely dangerous** to the watch painters.

....

....

b) The use of radium in a range of products went on for over **20 years**.
Explain why its use continued for so long.

....

....

....

Nuclear Power

Q1   The majority of the UK's electricity is still produced by burning **fossil fuels**.

a)   Is generating electricity using nuclear power a cheaper alternative to using fossil fuels?
Explain your answer.

....

....

b)   Write down **two** other **advantages** and **disadvantages** of nuclear power
compared to using fossil fuels to generate electricity.

Advantages: 1. ....

2. ....

Disadvantages: 1. ....

2. ....

c)   Explain why some people are **against** the use of nuclear power to generate our electricity.

....

....

....

Q2   **Radioactive waste** left over from **nuclear fission** is very difficult to dispose of.

a)   Why is the waste produced by nuclear power stations such a long-term problem?

....

....

b)   Vitrification is one way of disposing of radioactive waste.
Describe the process of vitrification.

....

....

c)   Why is nuclear waste usually buried deep underground?

....

....

Top Tips: Nuclear power is a tricky subject — there are arguments for and against it.
Make sure you know **both** sides of the argument. That way you can argue with yourself.

Mixed Questions — P2b Topics 4, 5 & 6

Q1 Nick and Rob go on a roller coaster. With them in it, the roller coaster carriage has a total mass of **1200 kg**.

a) At the start of the ride the carriage rises up to its highest point of **60 m** above the ground and stops. Calculate its gain in gravitational potential energy.

....

....

b) The carriage then falls to a third of its maximum height. Assuming there is no air resistance or friction, calculate the speed of the carriage at this point.

....

....

....

c) One of the carriages needs to be repaired. A super strong handyman pushes it 120 m from the ride to the repair workshop. Calculate the work done by the handyman, if he pushes the carriage with a constant force of 85 N.

....

....

Q2 The table gives information about four different **radioactive isotopes**.

a) Explain how the atomic structure of cobalt-60 ($^{60}_{27}$Co) is different from the structure of 'normal' cobalt-59 ($^{59}_{27}$Co).

....

....

Source	Type of Radiation	Half-life
radon-222	alpha	3.8 days
technetium-99m	gamma	6 hours
americium-241	alpha	432 years
cobalt-60	beta and gamma	5.27 years

b) Which sources in the table would be most suitable for each of the uses below?

....

  medical tracers   **smoke detectors**   **detecting leaks in pipes**

c) Radiation can be used to treat cancer. What type of radiation is used in this treatment?

....

d) Give **one** precaution that should be taken by industrial nuclear workers to protect themselves from radiation.

....

Mixed Questions — P2b Topics 4, 5 & 6

Q3 The diagram below shows part of a chain reaction in a nuclear reactor.

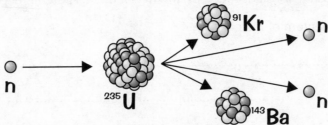

a) What is the name of the type of nuclear reaction shown in the diagram?

....

b) This decay happens as part of a chain reaction. Describe what happens in this chain reaction.

....

....

....

c) Explain how the following work to control the chain reaction in a nuclear reactor.

   i) Moderators: ....

   ....

   ii) Control rods: ....

   ....

d) What would happen if this reaction was not controlled?

....

....

e) Describe how thermal energy from the reactor is used to generate electricity.

....

....

f) Give one disadvantage of using nuclear power to generate electricity compared to other methods.

....

g) Nuclear **fusion** produces more energy than the process above.
Write down one of the conditions needed for fusion to take place.

....

Mixed Questions — P2b Topics 4, 5 & 6

Q4 Cherie and Tony rob a bank. They escape in a getaway car with a mass of **2100 kg** and travel at a constant speed of **90 km/h** along a straight, level road.

a) Calculate the momentum of the car.

....

....

b) A police car swings into the middle of the road and stops ahead of Cherie's car. Cherie slams on the brakes and comes to a halt **3.0 s** after she starts braking.

   i) Write down one factor that could affect Cherie's thinking distance.

   ....

   ii) Assuming the car decelerates uniformly, find the force acting on the braking car.

   ....

   ....

c) Explain how seat belts would have helped keep Cherie and Tony safer if they had crashed.

....

....

Q5 Fay measures the activity of a sample of pure copper-64 in her home, using a Geiger-Muller tube. The graph below shows her results.

a) Fay had previously measured the background rate to be 100 Bq. Find the half-life of copper-64.

....

....

....

....

....

b) She takes her Geiger-Muller tube to her friend's house and finds the background rate is much higher. Give one reason why the level of background radiation changes from place to place.

....

P2b Topic 6 — Using Radioactive Materials